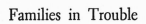

Families in Trouble

EARL LOMON KOOS

# Families
# in Trouble

*With a Preface by*
ROBERT S. LYND

NEW YORK / RUSSELL & RUSSELL

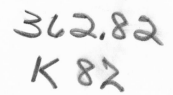

# Acknowledgments

THIS VOLUME is the result of an extended case study of a group of low-income urban families. The study was made during the years 1940–1943 under a grant for that purpose from the Josiah Macy, Jr. Foundation to the Department of Sociology in the Faculty of Political Science of Columbia University.

Two men are primarily responsible for the inception of this study. Without the stimulation and careful guidance of Professor Robert S. Lynd, my own interest in the problems of the low-income family would not have crystallized. Without the provocative encouragement of Mr. Lawrence K. Frank, then Executive Secretary of the Foundation, I would not have focused my thought upon the particular aspects of family life considered here, and without his interest in providing research funds the time could not have been allotted for the study.

Professors Wilbur C. Hallenbeck and Paul F. Lazarsfeld and Dr. Margaret Mead were helpful at various stages in the study, and Dr. Robert K. Merton gave freely of his time in the final stages of manuscript preparation.

I am especially indebted to Professor Edmund deS. Brunner for his interest and continuing help in the later stages of the study and during the preparation of the manuscript.

My thanks are also due my colleagues on the faculty of the University of Rochester and my former associates on the staff of the Rochester Council of Social Agencies for their criticisms and assistance in the final preparation of the manuscript.

My greatest debt is to the sixty-two families whose coöperation was whole-heartedly given, even though there must have been times when our conversations seemed to them endless and without point. Complete anonymity had been guaranteed the participants, but it was nevertheless not easy for these men and women to uncover their disappointments, their failures, conflicts and frustrations to the scrutiny of a stranger, especially when that stranger had no particular status in their community.

Earl Lomon Koos

Rochester, New York
January 10, 1946

# Preface

THE REVERSE SIDE of the American dream is woven of trouble. This is a thing we dont talk about, a thing Mr. Benton and the State Department will not export with their propaganda for "the American way." It is the vulnerable under-side of our vaunted individualism and opportunity, of our lack of social structure that heaps people together in cities and leaves them seeking vitality in massed rows of human anonymity at the movies. It is an important commentary on the American way that so many Americans can say with one of Mr. Koos' subjects, "I dont remember when I didn't have to worry." But "trouble," as used in this book, concerns more than the constant unraveling of life through worry. What Mr. Koos was after is the bigger jolts, when things let one down hard, and something must be done—at once; "when," to quote again from the book, "you've got no place—nobody—to turn to, and there don't seem to be any rules for doing anything about it." Presumably, an important test of a good society is how much preventable real trouble it removes from the shoulders of its citizens, and, after that, how rapidly and effectively it marshals what it knows to repair the damage done by non-preventable trouble.

A society as determined as ours to be optimistic imposes false-faces on all of us. Refugees in our midst from Central Europe find this American trait particularly difficult. For to the greeting "How are you?" the answer must be a confident and hearty "Fine!" In a more solidly built social order one belongs securely enough to one's fellows to be able to relax one's guard; but with us the simple human admission of discouragement and a troubled mind is often withheld from even our closest friends. In a culture in which to be unsuccessful means automatically to be in some wise a failure, one tends perforce to wrestle with one's black moods alone and unaided. Students of American marriage have stressed the intolerable burden which this sharp separation of outside world and inner private world behind one's shut front door places upon the fragile relations between husband and wife. And so great is the American fear of failure that, even within one's marriage, fatigue and discouragement may create dismay in the other person closest to one.

How many of us have at one time or another stopped dead in our tracks, momentarily paralyzed by the thought of the weight of human trouble in the homes packed into the single city block in which we happen to live—especially those grim appraisals of self that go on behind darkened windows when the wakeful lie wide-eyed and desperate asking over and over "What *can* I do about it?"

That is what Mr. Koos set out to discover within the compass of one city block. He was not looking for human tragedy. Rather, he posed the following situation: Here were people, tier upon tier of them, living in the five- and six-story flats confronting each other across a city street. Somewhere else—downtown, on other streets— were institutions set up to care for welfare, whose presence to care for people in trouble enables solid citizens in some measure to rationalize away the wreckage of an acquisitive society. Did the two —the troubles of people and the agencies set up to help people cope with their troubles—actually meet?

It will startle many to see how meagerly they do meet. What Mr. Koos finds is the thing we all know to be there but which few of us like to admit: a vast array of human trouble largely untouched by any and all of the resources for help set up by society. Despite social workers, pastors, city welfare departments, clinics, schools, the press and all of the other paraphernalia of a great city, the anxious words echo again and again from this block: "I need to know what to do." Welfare agencies are distant or unknown, or they terrorize by their brisk routine; while even churches grope remote from much of this inner human anguish: "Our pastor is a *good* man and he lives a good life, but I know he doesn't really know how I feel about not knowing what to do."

This particular block housed economically poor people; it was not picked as a bad area but as one of hundreds of blocks in New York City where families pay an average monthly rent of less than thirty dollars. More than half the male family heads were semi-skilled workers. But the study should not be read as the special case of "the poor." Because of our American emphasis on individual competence, "every tub on its own bottom," as a prime requisite for self-respect, it is precisely "the poor" who are best served by social-ized aids to competence in living. In the broad band of white-collar middle-class people above them, the American code attaches special shame to recourse to social agencies for aid. Not until one reaches the wealthy who can pay—and pay handsomely enough to be impersonal about it—for the services of child psychologists, psycho-analysts, lawyers, divorce courts and so on does seeking help become a relatively matter-of-fact affair. Wherever there is a middle class, there our type of society augments the fact of human trouble with an extra loading of social shame. The anxious distinction between "respectable" trouble and disgrace that Mr. Koos' study reveals tends to disappear among the middle class. There all human trouble except sickness and death is a thing to be kept secret.

One needs only to read these pages to realize what an exceptional interviewer Mr. Koos is. It takes good techniques and a superlatively genuine human being to be able to walk in on sixty-two families, unannounced and unsponsored, and to establish the kind of under-standing and confidence that prompts people to talk about the things in their lives that hurt most. His sensitive analysis of the causes and resultants of trouble both within and outside these families will be illuminating both to lay readers and to professional welfare workers. For all of us the book should serve as a jolting reminder of how little of what is needed is actually achieved by the present structure of social agencies.

But the problem of "trouble" dealt with in this book cuts far beneath "social work." It poses insistently for a democracy attempt-ing to get its living by the law of the jungle the following question: How long can we go on calling a system "democratic" that not only chronically breeds human trouble on such a colossal scale but also leaves constructive help so casually at the mercy of money and accident? R. H. Tawney has remarked that capitalist democracy operates to institutionalize inequality on a national scale. Nearly all of us have trouble sooner or later. The "inequality" lies in how soon, how often, and how helplessly beyond the reach of constructive assistance our troubles happen to us.

Robert S. Lynd

Columbia University
January 1946

# Contents

# Introduction

THE YEARS following 1929 have weighed heavily upon low-income families in this country. The clichés they have sworn by have proved to be empty phrases, and many have come to doubt their place in the present and their childrens' prospects for the future. It has been particularly in the great urban centers, where life is less softened by the amenities of neighborly friendship, that the maladjustments of our industrial society have tended to affect the low-income family. It is this group who pay an especially heavy price for our historic casualness about social organization.

Attempts to adjust low-income families to the exigencies of their environment are not new. Society has long recognized the need for such adjustment: settlements, charity organization societies—in fact, most social agencies—have developed as a result of this recognition. In recent years, with the depression reaching greater depths than had been thought possible, new techniques were created to deal with economic insecurity; for example, WPA, CCC, FSA—all simply letters of the alphabet in the early thirties—became symbols of society's new efforts to meet the need for adjustment on an economic level.

At best, however, these agencies aimed to buttress life against only a few of the most disturbing exigencies. The problems of adjustment have not been solved, for the needs of the low-income group are not merely for basic food and shelter but ramify widely through other economic needs and psychological necessities. Low-income urban families are more immediately affected by social change and more helpless because of their isolation and dependence upon others for food and the other necessities of life. Consequently, they find themselves confronted with problems which may well prove the complete undoing of their already poorly-knit social structure.

"Death and taxes are the only two things of which the poor can be certain." We can add an almost certain third: trouble. No one of these is, of course, confined to the low-income group. While trouble —at least the harsh, shattering kind with which we are concerned— in the life of the low-income urban dweller is our immediate concern in the present study, it is studied for the light it may throw upon the broad problem of urban living. If the phenomenon can be studied in the lives of the low-income urban group, with few protective barriers, inadequate resources, and little to lose, it seems not unlikely that the knowledge gained may also throw light upon equivalent problems on other income levels when stark emergency overtakes families.

Every research problem operates within the framework of an hypothesis. Ours may be stated as follows: there are problems—what we here call troubles—of urban families for which society has provided no particular means of solution or only solutions that lie beyond the level of income, education and sophistication of large numbers of families; these problems affect the structure and status of the family both as an interacting group and as a part of the community; as long as such problems fail of solution the individual and the family will be unable to carry out their functions adequately and human wastage will result.

The whole subject of the effects of the unusual and the unforeseen in the person's and the family's environment, especially when that environment makes constricting demands, has had little attention from the sociologist.[1] Where particular problems have been

1. Such attention as has been given to this subject has dealt largely with the effects of the depression upon families. Outstanding examples in this group are: Ruth S. Cavan and Katharine R. Ranck, *The Family and the Depression* (Chicago: University of Chicago Press, 1938); Robert C. Angell, *The Family Encounters the Depression* (New York: Charles Scribner's Sons, 1936). Noteworthy exceptions are the studies of bereavement by Thomas D. Eliot, *viz.* "The Bereaved Family," *Annals of the American Academy of Political and Social Science,* 160: 184–190; and by Howard Becker, *viz.* "The Sorrow of Bereavement," *Journal of Abnormal and Social Psychology,* 27: 391–410.

singled out the study has usually been based upon case records of social agencies.[2] This is not a criticism of such studies nor of this use of social case records. It is to say, however, that social agency records deal with troubles *in the process of treatment*, since treatment begins the moment the individual decides to approach the agency. Such investigations, therefore, have been concerned with selected groups of families, and possibly with selected groups of troubles.[3] For this reason the findings of such studies are not necessarily representative of any low-income population as a whole nor of the troubles of that population. Neither do they deal with the areas of life for which no specialized social services are available.

These are the aspects of the problem with which the present study is most concerned. Social agencies have been created to meet the bread-and-shelter problems of the low-income group. But it does not follow inevitably that all low-income families know about such agencies, will avail themselves of the services offered, or can meet the "entrance requirements" of the agencies. Nor is it definitely established that these agencies are prepared to serve all areas of human need, or for that matter that society is conscious of all such areas.

So far as we know, no earlier studies of family troubles have been made with this particular emphasis. The present study has attempted to avoid the limitations imposed by the use of social agency records through choosing the families to be studied without regard for previous agency contacts, and has likewise made the selection without regard for particular types of trouble.[4] The initial focus of the study has been upon the availability of social services to meet the troubles which have arisen, the knowledge of or ignorance of these services on the part of the family, and the attitudes of the

2. *Cf.*, for example, Katherine Lumpkin, *The Family: A Study of Member Roles* (Chapel Hill: University of North Carolina Press, 1936), which is based upon case records of the Charity Organization Society of New York.

3. Increasingly, social agencies make a non-generic approach to problems of human welfare. The development of excellent public welfare departments for the care of economic dependency, and the development of specialized forms of case work techniques have had much to do with this trend. Also, the whole tendency to "specialize" has probably contributed to this development.

4. The methods of selection and the techniques used are discussed in Chapter One: *The Methodology*, and in Appendix: *Interviewing in This Study*.

family toward such services. Also, the techniques used in the present study involved no authority such as is present in social case work situations, and it is therefore free from such influences. In these respects the study is probably unique.

The general question, how does a family solve or not solve its problems? has a concomitant question, What happens to the structure of the family when troubles occur? In other words, what internal stresses are set up, what changes in role evaluation take place because of the family's action or lack of action? Is the family less viable as a family because of the troubles to which it has been subjected? The literature on this subject is also limited, and suffers either from being based upon case studies of families which have sought the services of social agencies or upon studies of successful middle-class families. Because the two emphases are not unrelated, the present study has concerned itself with both, and two of the following chapters are devoted to a discussion of the family structure as it is affected by trouble.

The task of this research project has been, then, to study the lives of a group of low-income urban families; to note the troubles occurring during the period of the study, the efforts or lack of efforts of the families to solve the troubles; and to assay the changes in family structure and function—all with the hope that we may know, as a result, more about the techniques, the facilities, and the education needed to counteract trouble as it occurs in the lives of all of us.

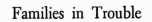
Families in Trouble

CHAPTER ONE

# The Methodology of the Study [1]

## THE CHOICE OF THE PROCEDURE

RESEARCH on the problem of family troubles may be conducted in several ways. One may identify a large number of troubles and treat them quantitatively, or a few troubles may be studied in great detail and treated qualitatively. Furthermore, one may study past troubles with the emphasis upon the most recent,[2] or attention may be directed solely to troubles occurring during the period of research. In the latter case there is a further choice: either to concentrate upon a single trouble in great detail or to study all troubles experienced by a family in a given period of time.

In this study the effort has been to concentrate upon all of the troubles experienced by the family over a period of time. This approach was chosen because it appeared to offer the best opportunity for studying the family's experiences *in toto*.

It was not possible, however, to disregard the effects of earlier troubles. A family's course of action in an earlier trouble situation

1. Pseudonyms are used in discussing families and in quoting individuals. While a similarity as to nationality has been maintained in the choice of the names, no other identification is to be construed.

2. If this is done, it involves the techniques used by Dr. Paul F. Lazarsfeld for studying the most recent (and presumably best remembered) instance in a series of similar events as a tool for market research. *Cf.* Paul F. Lazarsfeld, "Use of Detailed Interviews in Marketing Research," *Journal of Marketing*, 2:3–8 (1937).

might well exert an influence in a contemporary time of trouble,[3] and we have therefore to know as much about the earlier family life as possible. While the primary emphasis was upon all troubles occurring in the family during the period of the study, it was accompanied by this secondary emphasis upon earlier and possibly conditioning troubles.

### THE DIFFICULTIES CONFRONTING RESEARCH OF THIS TYPE

As Margaret Mead has pointed out, the social scientist often finds it necessary "to illuminate rather than to demonstrate" a thesis. Demonstration requires generalization, and assured generalizations are impossible in a small number of cases possessing a large number of variables and sub-variables. Furthermore, since it is impossible to control the variables affecting family life as the physical scientist controls the conditions of his experiments, we are often unable to do more than illuminate our thesis.

Complete anonymity was guaranteed the families from the first interview—a necessity in any study as highly personalized as this one. This immediately places a heavy burden upon the investigator, and lays his work open to all of the charges of subjectivism usually leveled at observational studies. He is automatically denied the use of multiple judgments for relief from some of the *onus probandi*, and he suffers from this handicap. The fact that the investigator recognizes the dangers is in itself a positive check, however, and it can only be said that in the present instance every effort was made to guard against bias and subjectivity.

From the beginning in a study such as this, the investigator is faced with the fact that he has no status in the neighborhood which he plans to study. He has not been asked to come; he has no favors to distribute; he has no connection with any agency or organization of which the families might have knowledge; he consequently hopes

3. This was the case in the Harper family, where the father had gone to a social agency for help in 1933 and had been rejected after an initial (and for him, a very painful) interview. This family thereafter rejected all social agencies upon the basis of that one experience.

to operate in the delicate field of personal relationships without authority for such operation.

In this as in other new areas of investigation, he has constantly to face the fact that he is traveling in territory for which no road maps exist. He is faced with uncertainty—with the necessity for exercising judgment at every turn, and that judgment with only erratic benefit of precedent. The fact that there are so many unexplored areas which might profitably be investigated adds to the general confusion, no matter how carefully the subject matter has been delimited. One is tempted to "mount his horse and ride off in all directions at once."

Finally the subject matter itself offers difficulty, since it deals with the subject of trouble—which means failure, and as Margaret Mead has said, "in the American culture trouble is not respectable and therefore something better not discussed."

### THE LOCALE OF THE STUDY

The general area of New York City in which this study was made was chosen because it had already been the scene of many studies in human relations. A well-known health demonstration,[4] many studies by members of the near-by Cornell University's College of Medicine, a number of studies supported by the Josiah Macy, Jr. Foundation, and an already available detailed analysis of the demography of the area [5]—all of these were available as contributions to the sum of knowledge that is profitable background material for a study such as this.

The study was made in this big-city area rather than in a small city or village for two reasons. The foundation supporting this study asked that it be made within the Kips Bay–Yorkville Health District as part of a larger effort to gather other than routine health and social data in this area. Also, it was the writer's conviction that a

4. C.-E. A. Winslow and S. Zimand, *Health Under the El* (New York: Harper and Brothers, 1937).

5. The writer's *Kips Bay-Yorkville, 1940* (New York: Cornell University's College of Medicine, Department of Public Health and Preventive Medicine, 1940).

big-city area, with less neighboring and more institutionalized anonymity, would afford the study a more vulnerable population with which to work, *i.e.*, that the factors operating in trouble situations would affect families more directly and hence be more readily identified.

New York City's "East Seventies" constitute an urban area in a state of flux. Lying between New York's "Gold Coast" (Fifth and Madison Avenues) on the West and the rapidly developing new "Gold Coast" (the East River Drive) on the East are blocks of five and six-story tenements. Predominantly German, Austrian, Hungarian and Czech in the past, the latter years have seen an infiltration of Irish, Italians, and still other nationality groups into the area. Today approximately one-third of the population is foreign-born.

In their drabness the tenements are relatively uniform. With a population density averaging more than two hundred persons per acre, and with more than one person per room in most tenements, the buildings are old, poorly lighted, poorly heated, and unventilated. The average rent was less than thirty dollars per month.

More than half of the gainfully-employed workers in this area are semi-skilled or are employed in one of the domestic services. With incomes little above the subsistence level, a population living under these circumstances could hardly have effective barriers against troubles.

Within this general area a representative city block was chosen.[6] By using population, health, and other data, including the 1940 census tabulations, a census tract was selected which was as devoid of extremes in its population variables as seemed possible to secure.[7] This initial selection was further refined through an examination of the individual blocks in the tract to avoid choosing one in which unusual conditions might affect the representativeness of its popula-

6. The term "city block" is intended to mean a "social block" rather than a "census block." The former indicates the two sides of a street between intersections, the latter an area of land bounded by streets.

7. Extremes avoided in this choice included having a population predominantly of one nationality, of one religious affiliation, or one with a badly skewed age distribution.

tion, or where life might be unduly influenced by the presence of a clinic, settlement, or other social agency.

The families were chosen not for any particular characteristics they might possess, nor as families known to social agencies, but because they happened to reside in this representative block.[8] The desired number of families had originally and arbitrarily been set at seventy-five, but when sixty-two had agreed to coöperate in the study and their first interviews had been recorded it was evident that this number would exhaust the full time of the investigator.

The most important consideration was, of course, that the family had to be willing to participate in the study. It was recognized that this willingness would immediately introduce a biasing factor of self-selection in that coöperating families might be a special group possessing special characteristics that were important to the study. Coöperative families might well be those with only minor troubles (which disrupt family life very little), or with only "respectable" troubles—especially those which place no onus upon the family members as individuals (*e.g.*, unemployment due to impersonal economic causes).[9] It was not improbable that whole types of troubles —the more personal, the more disruptive, or those countering the behavior norms of the family—might be missed because of the necessity for this willingness to coöperate. It was possible, on the other hand, that the coöperating families might possess greater insight and greater sensitiveness to the plight of their group, and be willing to coöperate for that reason.[10]

8. The families in the block were listed by name from a mailbox enumeration, and a random drawing was made from this list after families without children had been eliminated. Only families with one or more children were included because of the study's concern with intra-family structure.

9. It was the necessity for getting beyond the minor or "respectable" troubles which led to the adoption of the technique used. The single interview technique would be unlikely to uncover problems of any serious nature.

10. The writer considers that this was the reason for coöperation by a number of families, and that this was in part due to the way in which the families were approached. (see *infra*)

Since social research cannot create controlled family situations, it was possible only to recognize the probable existence of these negating factors. Therefore, the study can best be said to have been concerned with a spatially random, though somewhat self-selected, group of low-income urban families.

Eighty-one families were interviewed before the sixty-two which coöperated in the study were secured. The nineteen which refused were either antagonistic or indifferent. Twelve of the families refusing did so summarily, the others after some discussion. Only one of the nineteen was aggressively antagonistic.

Much information was gained about these families in the course of the study. Since the fact of refusal is important in considering the fact of coöperation, the following material concerning the families which refused is included here.

The aggressively antagonistic family (in which the father threatened to throw the investigator down the stairs) was one in which both parents had served jail terms for petty thievery. This family had nothing to do with any other family in the block.

The three families which made no response to the investigator's opening statement were all considered to be "a little queer" by other families in the block. Being "a little queer" in this area meant that the family kept to itself and restricted the children's activities to the family circle.

Of the seven families which refused to participate even after some discussion, four were later found to have been in one or another stage of trouble at the time of the interview. This withdrawal during trouble is discussed at length in a later chapter.

The writer learned to know five of the twelve families which refused summarily. Without exception they expressed regret at not having been more cordial to the investigator, and their reasons throw light upon the attitudes of the low-income group toward the outsider.

*We wanted to talk to you when you came to see us that time,*
*but we both learned as kids that you don't talk to strangers—that*

New York is full of con game guys who'll rip you, and anyway, that nobody gives a damn about you [native-born chauffeur].

I couldn't believe the story you told was true. Why should anybody be interested in my troubles? In this country, nobody cares—in my own country we didn't have much but everybody in my village was willing to share what he had anyway. Here who cares? Your next-door neighbor don't even speak to you here, so I couldn't think you really meant what you said [foreign-born Czech janitor].

Even if we haven't got much money, people think we're suckers. I don't know why, but the less you have the more somebody tries to take it away from you. There's always somebody banging at your door and trying to soak you with something. I thought you had some skin game up your sleeve—I've learned to say no to anybody who comes to my door [native-born sanitary inspector].

I thought you was a social welfare person, and boy, did we get a belly-full of them a couple of years ago. We had to try to get relief after I lost my job in the depression when I was sick, and Jeez, what a ride that gal took us for. You'd thought I'd committed a crime, the way she put the screws on me. So when you started in I thought you were a guy from that welfare office [native-born laborer].

These statements indicate that institutionalized anonymity, the impersonality of tenement life, the vulnerability of the poor in financial matters, and the underlying distrust of "the social welfare person," all operate to render the low-income person suspicious of the outsider. It seems reasonable that if the vulnerability of the poor operates in situations like this, it also operates where the family is beset by trouble and needs to turn to an outside source for help.

## WHAT ARE TROUBLES?

One of the most difficult problems confronting this study at its inception was that of defining a trouble. What was to be considered as trouble as contrasted with the ordinary exigencies of life? One of the first interviews threw light upon a possible differentiation between the two:

> *What do you mean when you talk about us getting into trouble? You can say we're always in trouble because Mamie and I always have to scratch for the rent, and for money to raise the kids—there just ain't money comin' in to go around. But that ain't the trouble: hell, we got that kind of thing all the time. Maybe you mean the kind of thing happening to you that kicks the guts out of you? Something that really belts you one?* [Harper]

Discussions with this informant and with others bring to light certain of their ideas of what trouble does and does not involve. First, as this group knows it, trouble is accompanied by more than simple worry. Worry about whether or not the rent can be paid or new shoes purchased is so usual a component of life that it is accepted as something without which life is not real or complete.

> *Christ, I don't remember when I didn't have to worry. My worries started, I guess, the day we stood in front of the priest to be married, maybe before. I don't remember any time my father didn't worry either. But that's not being in a jamb—there's more to being in a jamb than worrying about every day things* [Graves].[11]

Worry is of course a concomitant of trouble, but from the discussions it was apparent that other elements bulk larger than does worry. One of these was a feeling of sharpened insecurity—over and above that feeling of insecurity always present for this group—which accompanied troubles. This was indicated by many families, and is shown in this typical statement:

> *The thing that gets you when you're in trouble is that you've got no place, nobody to turn to. You're just left hanging in the air. It's like dreaming you're falling from a building. You get just sick, and it's all because you've got nothing to stand on. You can worry it out about being short of dough when the rent's due, but somehow you make out as long as you have your job. But get into*

11. "Jamb" is the word most frequently applied to troubles by this group.

*a jamb, and you're shot, the bottom's clear out of things, it takes you a long time to get over it. And you don't know where to turn for help—that's part of it, too. A jamb is something you aren't used to handling,* and there don't seem to be any rules for doing anything about it [*Martin*].

The significance of the latter part of this statement should not be overlooked. This demand by trouble situations for new patterns of behavior is of primary importance in this study since cultural and other barriers may well prevent the family from adjusting itself to new configurations of behavior.

Troubles, then, are situations outside the normal pattern of life— situations which create a sharpened insecurity or which block the usual patterns of action and call for new ones. But troubles may involve more than these. Where troubles affect the intra-family relationships of the members, the respective positions of the members of the family may suffer temporary or permanent displacement as a result of trouble.

To the family there is no great difference between the exigency and the trouble. Both are part of the daily task of living, both are problems to be met. It must be realized that the difference between the two is primarily one for this study. These families deal with life on one level only, ordinarily—the level that permits one to exist as best he can under most undesirable circumstances.

It was foreseen that no two families would necessarily react to a given situation in the same way or with the same effect. What might be an ordinary exigency in life for one person or family could well be trouble for a second.[12] This possible variance in attitudes among families necessitated extreme care in designating the events in the life of each family which could be considered troubles. To the individual who experiences them, troubles and exigencies are much the same thing—the differentiation is our own and for purposes of analysis only.

12. Compare the experience of the Czabot family, where almost complete disorganization resulted from the gonorrheal infection of the sixteen-year-old son, with that of the patient in the clinic waiting room who said to the writer, "Hell, I'd just as soon have a dose of clap [gonorrhea] as a hard cold."

### THE EMPHASIS OF THE STUDY

Research concerned with family life is always confronted with the multi-faceted nature of the family. To overcome some of the obvious difficulties presented, the inquiry was focused upon the types of over-all reaction patterns that resulted from troubles and crises.

It was learned early in the first interview that a major effect of trouble in that particular family lay in changes in the dominance pattern, *i.e.*, in the relative authority exercised by each member of the family. As the study continued, this effect showed itself to be a major result of trouble in all families. For this reason, particular emphasis was placed upon this aspect of family life, and is discussed in detail in Chapter Six.

### THE ADEQUACY OF FAMILY ORGANIZATION

As the study passed through its planning stages, it was realized that not all families have the same degree of organization, and that the degree might well affect their ability to solve troubles and crises. Some families would be well-integrated, smoothly functioning, while others would be readily subject to a high degree of disorganization. Between these two extremes would probably be found a majority of the families with their organization adequate on some levels of life and much less so on others. The question also presented itself as to whether or not there was a relation between "trouble proneness" and the inadequacy of the family. Were the families which were always "in hot water" (and every social agency knows such families) in that state partially because of the inadequacy of their organization?

The difficulty of establishing concepts of adequacy as they pertain to family life are discussed by Cavan and Ranck:

> *The concepts of families as organized or disorganized, integrated or unintegrated, and adaptable or unadaptable are more or less intuitively arrived at by a consideration of a number of characteristics of family life. They are at best only an attempt to denominate a resultant of factors interacting in the process of family*

*life. None of these terms can explain why one family is organized or integrated and another is disorganized or unintegrated.*[13]

Despite the difficulty of assigning definite values to families as to their adequacy of organization, it seemed unavoidable that such an assignment be made if the relation of family adequacy to trouble and crisis was to be established. Keeping the difficulty constantly in mind, four criteria were established to gauge the degree of the family's adequacy of organization. These criteria were concerned entirely with intra-family relationships, which immediately raises the question of the family's function as such in the community. It was thought from the beginning (and confirmed by the early interviews) that if a family had an adequate intra-family organization, its relations with other families would also be adequate. For this reason, no criteria were employed to measure inter-family relationships.

The four criteria for obtaining an appraisal of the family's adequacy of organization were as follows:

1. There must be a consciousness of and acceptance by each member of his roles in the family, and also individual consciousness of and acceptance by each of the complementary roles of the other members of the family.

2. The family members must have a willingness to accept some common definition of the good of the family in preference to the good of the individual members. This willingness, too, must be one based upon mutual acceptance rather than coercion, for the coerced individual, while he may outwardly ascribe to the demands of the family, can hardly be said to be an integrated part of that family.

3. The members must find satisfaction within the family unit. This is not to say that all of the individual's needs must be met within and only within the family; the limitations of urban living for the low-income groups are such as to make this impossible. It is to say, however, that the adequate family must provide the normal satisfactions of family life sufficiently to prevent the individual's being *forced* to go outside the family to attain them.

4. The family must have a sense of direction and be moving in

13. Cavan and Ranck, *op. cit.*, p. ix.

keeping with this to however small a degree. This means that the family must be a "going concern," with an accepted sense of direction shared by its members. Unless a family can look to the future, to the attaining of new goals for itself and its members, its existence is a vegetative one and without purpose.

Having set these four criteria—the negative reporting was of course an indication of inadequacy—it was possible to place each family, at least approximately, in the range from complete adequacy to complete inadequacy. In subsequent chapters this range of adequacy will be used in discussing the relation of the organization of the family to the frequency of trouble, the methods of dealing with trouble, and the effects of trouble.

### THE FAMILY ROLES

One important effect of troubles upon family life is in terms of shifts in role evaluation. In our culture at the present time family roles are not firmly fixed, but are undergoing modifications to meet the exigencies of particular patterns of existence.[14] It is difficult for this reason to make any categorical statements as to roles, but in general the following are in effect. The man in the family occupies the roles of provider and head of the family. These are subject to great variations among families in urban areas, and have undergone changes in both. By and large, however, it is safe to say that man's

14. For the sake of clarity, the following definitions of status, role, and role evaluation are offered as used in this study: *Status,* a culturally determined position in the pattern of family life. *Role,* the dynamic aspect of a status, *i.e.,* how the individual puts the rights and duties of his status into effect. *Role evaluation,* the adequacy of the performance of the individual's rights and duties in his role as estimated by the other members of his family. A further distinction should be made between social and personal roles. The *social* role is one which has grown out of the past experience of the cultural group, *e.g.,* the role of breadwinner in the American family is a culturally-determined role ordinarily assigned the husband. The *personal* role is one which is determined by the individual and personal experiences of childhood; *e.g.,* the husband, if acting like a dependent child in his relationships with his wife and family, is exercising a personal role.

The definition of role and status are adapted from Ralph Linton, *The Study of Man* (New York: Appleton-Century, 1936), p. 113 f. The distinction between social and personal roles is adapted from Ruth S. Cavan, *The Family* (New York: Crowell, 1942), p. 167 f.

traditional role of provider remains, and that his authority as husband and father is still a potent force for control in the family life. The woman's roles are traditionally those of homemaker and mother. While the former has been subject both to additions and subtractions, it is also probably safe to say that there has been less displacement of the woman's roles in the American low-income urban family than in the case of the roles of the man.

The roles of the children are less easily characterized, since they are subject to change and are dependent upon many factors. They are primarily subordinate ones, but a subordination that is dependent in its degree upon the child's age, sex, sibling position, economic contribution to the family, the family's position in the community, and the changing concepts of the parents' relation to their children. This subordination continues at least until the adolescent years when the child may become an economic asset to the family. He may, however, usurp in varying degree roles previously held by the parents, especially when contribution to the family budget is a condition of the child's remaining in the family beyond the time of his becoming self-supporting. Shifts in the subordinate roles are likely to occur, also, in cases where foreign-born parents do not adapt readily to the American culture pattern, and the child becomes the chief liaison agent for the family as a whole.

There are, of course, exceptions to this pattern.[15] In families where

15. Evidence of the existence of these roles in this group of families is found in the attitudes and situations encountered. "It's the man's business to earn a living for his family." "Woman's job is running the home." "A man's got his work to do—a woman's got her's to do—that's only right." In these families, when the children are very small, the mother usually assumes a major role in training the child, but this is abrogated increasingly as the child grows older, and especially when the time comes for the father's heavy hand in matters of discipline. (This is especially true where there are boys in the family; girls continue to be trained and disciplined by the mother to a large extent.) Witness the frequency of the expression "Wait till your father comes home—he'll settle you!" However, even when the children are very young the final decision most often must wait upon the father in matters of importance (*e.g.*, as to whether or not the clinic shall be allowed to remove the child's tonsils).

In the case of the child's role, while the "children should be seen and not heard" concept has been pretty well abandoned, there still remains for most of these families the idea that "she's too young to know what's good for her."

chronic illness, a broken home, or any other unusual situation develops, it is not unlikely that the roles will be different. This, however, need not affect the adequacy of organization as long as the roles are held in a state of equilibrium, *i.e.*, as long as they meet the first of our criteria of adequacy—the recognition of and acceptance of the roles of the several members.

### THE PATTERNS OF VALENCE [16]

Of some concern to this study, also, are the special relationships which exist within families, and which may be displaced by troubles. These are especially important where a particular valence (*e.g.*, between the mother and a child) provides a means of sublimating the needs of a parent which are unmet because of the inadequacy of the family's organization. The continuance of accepted role evaluations may well be affected by changes in the valence patterns under such circumstances. Any study of the family in trouble must include such items if the picture of family inter-relationships is to be complete.

### ROLE EVALUATIONS

The individual's ability to perform his various roles is constantly subject to the scrutiny of the several members of the family. As a result, the individual's roles have as many evaluations as there are members in the family, and these are all subject to change as his performance in the roles changes. As the family undergoes the experience of trouble, these evaluations may undergo changes, depending upon the focus of the responsibility for the trouble or for its solution. (For example, if the father is responsible for the trouble or for failing to provide a solution, the mother's evaluation of his performance of his roles may be depressed.) Changes in role evaluation occur frequently in family life, especially where there is inadequate organization, and are barometers of family inter-action.

Certain of the roles are presumably less subject to devaluation

16. Defined for our purposes as the special relationships that exist within families, as for example, the special attachment of the mother for one particular child.

than others since they are more rigidly fixed by the culture. For example, the role of breadwinner is relatively fixed in the subculture of which these families are members. The wage (a measure of the individual's ability to fill that role) is determined not so much by the individual's own wishes as by factors in the culture as a whole (scarcity of labor, etc.). This role is therefore less subject to devaluation, even when the breadwinner experiences unemployment (except in cases where unemployment is due to personal failure rather than to economic causes).

In the case of the role of disciplinarian, much more depends upon the personal abilities of the individual—it is therefore more subject to devaluation. In the Fratise family, the father described his evaluation of his own father's role in the following words:

> *My old man never earned much money. But how the hell could he, when you live in a big city where they don't pay any more than they do? He always kept us fed and with clothes on our backs and we had a place to sleep, and we didn't need any more than that. As a provider, my old man was* ALL RIGHT. *But, Jesus, wasn't he a rotten father in some other ways! When I was a.kid we never knew if he was going to bat us around or give us a nickel for a drink. We used to hate like hell to see him come home.*

The evaluation of each individual's roles and the devaluations resulting from trouble must therefore be considered in terms of the collective evaluation of these roles by the other members of the family.

### DETAILS OF THE RESEARCH TECHNIQUE

The nature and extent of the study made it impossible to utilize a rigid schedule or questionnaire. The interviews proceeded within a pre-established framework of questions which were applicable to all of the families.[17] In the next few pages some of these questions are given as indications of the approaches that were made in determin-

17. The basic suggestions for these questions were obtained from Caroline Zachry-Margaret Mead, *Suggestions For Working Out The Backgrounds For Case Studies On Adolescents.* Unpublished Mss.

ing the effects of the troubles, and the reasons for the particular effects.

With a high incidence of foreign-born and native-born-of-foreign-
born parents in the neighborhood, possible troubles had to be considered in their relation to the cultural heritage of the families. Two
families of different ethnic stock but having approximately the same
gross characteristics might react in entirely different ways to a
trouble situation because of the differences in their earlier cultural
patterns. The following are examples of the questions used in determining this carry-over: How much of the old-world language was
used in the home? Was it used in place of English, in conjunction
with it, and under what circumstances was it resorted to in the latter
case? Which of the old-world customs were retained in family life
here, and how was their retention rationalized? Were the old-world
customs employed constantly, reserved for special occasions, or used
only for display? What contacts had the family made in the city to
continue the use of the old-world patterns? What contacts had the
family made to strengthen the old-world culture heritage for the
second and third generations?

Before any evaluation could be made of changes in roles and
valences, the patterns for each family had to be determined. What
were the roles of each of the family members? If they did not follow
the usual pattern, how and why were they different? What valences
existed within the family? What factors operated to establish these
special patterns, if they were unusual?

Other questions to be answered before the family pattern could
be indicated were of the following order: Who earned the living, or
supplemented it? Who handled the money in the family? Whose
discipline was most effective? Who deferred to whom in conversation? Who assumed the responsibility for making decisions on the
several levels of family activity? Who did the buying? Who chose
the place of residence? What child was most favored by each parent,
and for what reasons?

Other questions dealt with the reasons for these relationships.
Were they determined by the cultural heritage? Were they of a
temporary or permanent nature? Were the role evaluations and

valences willingly or resentfully accepted? Were they rebelled against, by whom, and with what results?

All of these questions and many more of a similar nature were necessary if it was to be possible to approximate the position of each individual in the family, and to recognize the relation of each member of the family to the other members.

Similarly, a number of questions demanded answers concerning the methods of solving troubles. Did relatives, friends, neighbors provide help? Did the community afford potential institutionalized help for the family in solving its troubles? Was it ignorance of potential sources of help that made families bungle the handling of their troubles? Were there connotations surrounding actual sources of help that prevented the family from making use of them? Were there troubles that were outside the area of family self-help, and for which there were no institutionalized services available?

Many questions had to be answered in the case of each trouble in a family to evaluate these aspects of the problem. What kinds of services were needed to meet the particular problem? Were there channels by means of which the family could be expected to have heard of the service? These questions could be answered only through an investigation of the social service offerings in the neighborhood, and this was done by the writer. Did the family actually know of the availability of the services? If they did know of them, what were the reasons for not using them? These questions were answered through asking the family to identify the agencies which could reasonably be expected to offer the service, and where they were able to identify them, the reason for their refusal to seek help. (This, of course, was done at the end of the study—not during the course of the observation.)

When it became clear that an event constituted a trouble rather than just an exigency, and with the family pattern outlined in detail, it was less difficult to indicate what happened to the family in trouble. In the evaluation of the trouble period, questions similar to the following had to be answered: How did the role evaluations shift? What changes occurred in the role patterns? Did the valence pattern shift, and why?

Regarding the post-trouble situation, the following questions are representative of the inquiry made: Did the old patterns reassert themselves? Were losses in role evaluation apparent? Were they permanent, immediately restored, or slow in returning to their former level? Were there definite gains in any role evaluations as a result of satisfactory solutions of the troubles?

Difficulty was expected when the effects of an earlier trouble might not have been completely resolved before a second or even a third trouble occurred. In such cases there were special difficulties in determining losses and gains in role evaluations. Only by an involved system of bookkeeping for each member of the family and for each event was it possible to determine such changes and their relation to particular troubles. By recording each trouble separately and entering observations concerning the effects of that trouble upon separate cards for each member of the family, however, the records were kept from becoming hopelessly involved.

Knowledge of what happened to the family in its community relationships as a result of trouble depended largely upon a knowledge of the family's integration into the community. Through questioning and observation the family's patterns of social intercourse were charted and the frequencies of contacts noted. Special attention was paid to the relationships involving other families, and the age and social levels at which these relationships operated were carefully noted. Having established these indices for each family, the following questions were applicable: Were these social routines affected by the trouble? Did the family react by withdrawing from certain contacts, and from which ones? Were there increases in the frequency of certain contacts as a result of, or during trouble?

The families were not prepared in any way for the first visit. The first call was made when it was expected that the father and mother would both be at home. While the names were known, having been drawn from the list, the family's name was not used. The investigator introduced himself as an individual who was interested in talking with the family about the jambs which occur in city family life.

He explained that he was interested in how social agency services could be bettered, and that the coöperation of the family was desired for this reason. It was explained that he represented no institution, was in fact a graduate student at Columbia University, and did not expect to gain anything from this except knowledge that might help straighten out present difficulties. Since projection and identification play an important part in establishing rapport, an effort was made early in the interview to have the respondents identify the writer with themselves through the casual introduction into the conversation of an account of a trouble in the interviewer's life.[18] This initial sharing of experiences with the family did much to break down barriers which ordinarily exist. Every effort was made, at the same time, to keep obvious differences of speech, dress, and manner at a minimum.

No attempt was made to secure detailed information about the family at the first interview. Nor were family members expected to think of it as anything but an isolated interview. It was realized that many interviews (and over an extended period of time) would be needed if the reaction of the family to trouble was to be known. Such a program was too ambitious to introduce to the family at the first interview; the amount of rapport that could be obtained at a first interview was ordinarily insufficient to permit asking for a series. The investigator did ask, however, at the close of each preliminary interview, if he might think over what the family had told him and then come back if additional questions occurred to him.

The major purpose of the first interview was to have the family know the individual as *a human being with problems of his own*, and as one who could be trusted with their confidences. This general approach was made because of the writer's belief that too many research workers, in their pursuit of fact, forget the human values inherent in a face-to-face research situation such as this.

18. At the time of undertaking the study the writer's wife was in a hospital in a serious condition. This fact was brought into the conversation at the earliest opportunity by saying "I know how I feel when I'm in a jamb—my wife is in the hospital now. How do you feel in a situation like this?"

It was made plain from the outset that absolute anonymity was guaranteed not only for the period of the study but permanently.[19] The validity of the personal approach, and of the guarantee of anonymity was established later by the statement of several family members.

> *We talked it over after you left the first time. Norah said you seemed like a decent guy with troubles of your own and she sorta liked to talk to you. I said "Hell, he won't hurt us any if he keeps his mouth shut and I guess he will. I'm willing to talk to him again if it'll help any." Fact is, we were kinda glad to see you come back.*

> *Mina and I figured maybe we shouldn't talk with you again, just say we'd changed our minds. Then I remembered your telling about your wife being in the hospital and the mess you were in, so I said "If he can open up like that, I guess I can, too." Anyway, you'd promised nobody'd ever know what we told you.*

A different value inherent in this "conscious technique of being a human being" is indicated in a later statement by the wife in one family.

> *It was good just to talk to somebody who understood—to tell the truth and not worry if the relief [the Department of Welfare Investigator] would be mad because we did what we did. Why wouldn't we talk about how troubles make our lives different, when we know it wouldn't hurt us?*

Most of the families, despite their surface acceptance of the study, needed to be visited more than once before the necessary degree of rapport was established. Here, too, a later statement was revealing.

> *You see, it isn't easy to be honest with a stranger. We had to feel you weren't a stranger, but we still felt it the second time you came. Then, when you talked about your house in the country and*

19. The guarantee has been kept. Checking with the families, fifty-seven of which could be located seventeen months after the close of the field work period, showed that no family had any cause for concern in this respect.

*how you raised your own food and all, it just seemed we didn't see
a stranger when we saw you again [Czabot: on the third visit].*

When rapport had been established, the first focus was upon the
last trouble which had occurred in the life of the family. By this approach the investigator learned what the family considered to be
trouble, and what their reaction to trouble was. The retrospective
approach also made possible an early insight into the structure of
the family, and clarified the observations made in the first interview
or two regarding role evaluations and the valence patterns.

While this retrospective approach offered these initial advantages,
it also served another important purpose. As was mentioned earlier,
the observation of reactions during the field work period would
hardly be sufficient, since the family's course of action might well
have been conditioned by troubles antedating that period. As a prac-
tical matter, based upon the experience with the first few families, it
was found necessary not only to cover in detail the last previous
trouble but also to secure as detailed data as possible on the major
troubles of the family from its beginning. The completeness of these
data varied from family to family, especially as the age of the family
increased, but on the whole they provided fairly complete descriptions of the earlier years and of significant events in those years.

After the details of the last previous trouble had been secured, and
a detailed picture obtained of the structure of each family, the investigator kept in regular contact with the families through visits to the
home or through other contacts as often as the situation demanded.
Each family was kept under study for the full period of the investigation (two years) with one exception—one family moved away
from New York City sixteen months after the first interview.

In the families where troubles were non-existent or infrequent,
the visits were less regular. In times of trouble visits were made as
often as the individual situation permitted. In at least one family,
contacts were made as frequently as six times in one week with different members of the family during a period of trouble. The
friendly, non-professional nature of the visits made it possible to see
the family without unduly sensitizing its members to the trouble

situations. Also, the interviewer made a point of never allowing himself to seem to be hunting for troubles to talk about. The problem of recurring visits was therefore not difficult to handle.[20]

The reader may well ask himself why such a rete of questions need have been answered if the effect of troubles upon family life was to be known. The answer can only be that a detailed knowledge of what happens in human lives can only be had through a detailed knowledge of how those humans live. Not every answer to every question is treated in the following pages, but every answer to every question went in some measure into the judgment of what happened to the family in a given situation.

This study, then, involved a qualitative examination of the effects of troubles upon the lives of a group of low-income urban families. The pattern of family organization was first ascertained, the last trouble was discussed, and the investigator then continued his study of the family through the two-year period, observing the troubles which occurred, the ways in which the families attempted to meet them, and the intra- and inter-family effects of those troubles.

We can look now at the question, who were these families, what were their characteristics, how did they live?, and then proceed in later chapters to a discussion of just how the information indicated above was used.

20. *Cf.* Appendix.

# CHAPTER TWO

# The Families Studied

ANY understanding of the effect of trouble upon the lives of these sixty-two families depends in part upon having a general understanding of the environment, of the patterns of living, and of the general characteristics of the families.[1]

## THE ENVIRONMENT

The general layout of the New York City tenement areas will be familiar to the reader. There are no front yards—the buildings begin at the sidewalks; there are no open spaces between buildings—only irregular small courts through which light and air seek their way to the lower floors. Areaways are interposed between the tenements facing on adjacent streets, but these provide little more than a place for clotheslines. Where the family is able to pay the extra rent for a front tenement, they may look out upon the street—otherwise they have either of two views: the half-filled milk bottles and the window "ice boxes" of the folk across the court, or the neighbor's washing hanging in the rear areaway.

Some of the tenements are "railroad flats," which means that the rooms are strung together one behind the other like cars on a track. The family living in such a tenement has both street and areaway

1. These descriptions are somewhat disguised. Some details have been described with changes in minor identifying features sufficient to prevent possible identification of specific families. In no case has the essential meaning been destroyed.

exposures, but pays high rents for the added space and ventilation and light. It is a slight handicap to have to go through all of the rooms to get from the front of the tenement to the back, but such a handicap is unimportant when compared with other problems of tenement living.

The bathroom—more than half of the families have one—may be anywhere that architectural convenience dictated. It may open off the kitchen—it did open off the living room in one instance. In the older buildings it has very often been placed in the hall as an afterthought, where it is shared with one or more families. It does not, in every case, include facilities for bathing.

With space at a premium, the kitchen most often serves as dining room, laundry, general storeroom and utility room. Bedrooms usually serve a dual purpose—as sleeping quarters and as storage rooms, and have the least desirable exposure and hence the least ventilation. Rarely does one person occupy a bedroom by himself.

In such an environment there is little or no privacy. With less than one room per person, there is little chance for the individual to be alone, either with his possessions or his thoughts. These buildings with thin walls and floors afford no privacy from the ears of the neighbors, and voices raised in times of trouble can easily be heard in adjoining tenements; nor is there any way of shutting out the sounds and smells originating in neighboring tenements.[2] In the words of one of the fathers who had recently taken his children to the Central Park Zoo, "We have just as much privacy as the sea lions in the park."

THE PATTERN OF LIVING

Coupled with the necessity for living under conditions such as these is the equally difficult problem of the *immediacy of living*. As the investigator strips off the outer layers of low-income urban existence he becomes increasingly aware of its hand-to-mouth quality.

2. For a discussion of the effect of such living conditions upon the individual, see James S. Plant's section on "Crowding and the Individual" in his *Personality and the Cultural Pattern* (New York: The Commonwealth Fund, 1937), pp. 213–228.

Only the things that must be done managed to get done. There are no sheltered reservoirs within which man can store up his surplus thoughts, energies, and products—and not surprisingly, because for people living under these conditions there are no surplus thoughts and energies and products. They need all of their energies and every cent they can earn in order to meet the day-by-day demands, and they know that their environment will make endless demands upon them whichever way they turn. Life under such conditions takes on a nip-and-tuck urgency that belies our culture's middle-class *ethos* of a reasoned calculation of one's future.

Individuals and whole families of individuals suffer from these pressures. Housewives lament that they can buy only for the next meal because there is no place in which to store additional foods. Wage earners know that every cent they make is mortgaged in advance simply to keeping up with basic expenditures, and they curse and worry because they cannot save for a rainy day. Adolescent girls have no place in which to entertain the "boy friend" because home offers no opportunity for privacy. Only the youngest members of the family can dawdle and dream beyond life's immediacies, and they, too, suffer indirectly.

The reader will say that these pressures exist for all urban dwellers, and that to a degree they characterized the whole of the American culture. This is undoubtedly true, but the fact remains that in a money-centered culture such as ours these effects are ameliorated—in part, at least—when the individual or family has money enough to exercise some choices and to make some plans. In the low-income group here under study, which lacks adequate means of meeting these demands, the effect is likely to be severe, if not critical.

### CHARACTERISTICS OF THE FAMILIES

One of the important conditions was that the study be made among a population that was representative—in other words, that the families studied not be of one nationality, age group, or other characteristic. One of the evidences of a satisfactory group of families for study is found in their polyglot nature.

*Nationality and Nativity:*

Of the sixty-two families studied, thirty-five (56.5 percent) were native-born.[3] Of these thirty-five, however, twenty-nine (46.8 percent of the total) were native-born-of-foreign-born-parents, and thus were only one generation removed from an old-world culture. The latter included Czechs, Irish, Germans, Italians, Hungarians, Poles, Scots, and Belgians. Of the remaining twenty-seven families with foreign-born heads, twenty-one had a single old-world culture pattern, *i.e.*, with no intermarriage of nationalities. Table I shows the distribution of the families by the nativity and nationality of the father.

TABLE I

*Distribution of Families by Nativity and
Nationality of Fathers*

| Nativity and nationality | Number | Percent |
|---|---|---|
| Native-born: | | |
| of native parents | 6 | 9.7 |
| of foreign-born parents | 29 | 46.8 |
| Foreign-born: | | |
| German | 7 | 11.2 |
| Irish | 7 | 11.2 |
| Czechoslovakian | 6 | 9.7 |
| Italian | 4 | 6.5 |
| Hungarian | 1 | 1.6 |
| Danish | 1 | 1.6 |
| English | 1 | 1.6 |

If we add together the foreign-born and native-born-of-foreign-born-parents, the study was concerned with six native-born families in which any old-world cultural patterns had been so diluted as to be indistinguishable, and with the following nationalities in the frequencies indicated:

| | |
|---|---|
| Czechoslovakian | 14 |
| Irish | 14 |
| German | 13 |
| Italian | 6 |
| Hungarian | 3 |
| English, Scotch, Belgian, Danish, Austrian, and Polish | 1 each |

3. All families are classified by the characteristics of the father.

The foreign-born members of the families were relatively uniform in their agrarian backgrounds. Two of the Germans, one of the Czechs, two of the Irish, and the English and Danish family heads had urban backgrounds before migrating to the United States. With the exception of the Dane, all had low-income status in Europe. The remaining foreign-born had been reared either in small villages or in the open country, and identified themselves as peasants in their respective countries.

Of the twenty-seven foreign-born families, twenty had fathers who were naturalized, and the fathers of two more had taken out their first papers. The incidence of naturalization among the foreign-born women was somewhat lower. It is worth noting that failure to avail themselves of the privilege of naturalization occurred most often among the group from Southern and Eastern Europe, and in those families where the lack of education was most obvious.

### Residential Mobility:

The length of time these families had lived where first interviewed varied greatly (see Table II). One family had lived in the same tenement for more than fifteen years, others had moved three, four, or five times in the last ten years—one had lived at nine addresses in eight years. The length of time the family had resided where first studied is of importance since light is thrown upon their possible knowledge of social services in the immediate area and of the "neighboring" which might be expected to occur if the families had continued at one address long enough to have put down "grass roots." That the families as a group were fairly stable is indicated by the

TABLE II

*Length of Time at Address Where First Studied*

|  | No. | Cumulative Percent |
|---|---|---|
| More than 15 years | 1 | — |
| 10 to 15 years | 8 | 14.5 |
| 5 to 10 years | 6 | 24.2 |
| 2 to 3 years | 24 | 63.0 |
| 1 to 2 years | 18 | 92.0 |
| 6 months to 1 year | 4 | 98.5 |
| Less than six months | 1 | 100.0 |

fact that approximately one-fourth had resided at the address where first interviewed for more than five years, and that almost two-thirds had lived there for more than two years. Of the five which had lived in "the block" less than one year, four had lived within a two-block radius prior to that time—the fifth within six blocks. It is apparent, therefore, that none of these families were strangers to the area or labored under any special handicap from not having had time to form neighborhood friendships.

*Size of Family and Age of Parents:*

The distribution of the families by size and composition as related to the age of the parents is shown in Table III.[4] Since the age of the father and mother did not differ greatly in any family, the ages used are those of the fathers. This age of parents is of importance since it

TABLE III

*Size and Composition of Families as Related to the Age of the Parents*

| Composition of family | Under 30 | Age Group 30–40 | 40–50 | Over 50 | Total |
|---|---|---|---|---|---|
| Parents, one child | 5 | 11 | 1 | 1 | 18 |
| Parents, two children | 6 | 14 | 8 | 1 | 29 |
| Parents, three children | — | 3 | 5 | — | 8 |
| Parents, four children | — | 1 | 1 | — | 2 |
| Parents, one child, one collateral | — | 1 | — | — | 1 |
| Parents, two children, one collateral | — | 1 | 1 | — | 2 |
| Parents, one child, one grandparent | 1 | 1 | — | — | 2 |
| Total | 12 | 32 | 16 | 2 | 62 |

is quite possible that younger parents, not yet firmly set in their family patterns, would be better able to meet the impact of trouble than would older and more stable parents (or *vice versa*). The relation of age of parents as it affects their handling of troubles will be discussed in a later chapter.

4. It should be remembered from Chapter One that only complete families, *i.e.*, with both parents and at least one child, were approached in setting up the study group.

*Family Income and Expenditures:*

The range of family incomes varied from twenty-two dollars per week to more than fifty dollars (see Table IV). For the most part the earnings were steady, even though scant. The soft drink salesman was the only one whose income varied greatly through the year. It should be noted here that the time of the study (1941–1943) was fortunate in that the bitter conditions of the depression years had been alleviated and the heightened wages and living costs due to the war had not yet appeared.

The total family expenditures matched, and sometimes exceeded, the family income. Forty-nine (79.0 percent) were on an income-equals-outgo basis; five (8.1 percent) were able to save small amounts, either through insurance or with bank accounts; the remaining eight (12.9 percent) gradually accumulated debts. These are all discussed later as they relate to the family's way of dealing with troubles.

TABLE IV

*Distribution of Total Family Income from All Sources*

| Less than $22.50 per week | 3 |
|---|---|
| 22.50 to 27.50 | 31 |
| 27.50 to 32.50 | 14 |
| 32.50 to 37.50 | 8 |
| 37.50 to 42.50 | 4 |
| 42.50 and over | 2 |
| Total | 62 |

Some families budgeted their incomes strictly, some simply drew from the family purse until it was empty and then waited for the next date of income. One family managed to keep going with the assistance of the "six-for-five boys," [5] and with help from the jewelry loan racket.[6] One was constantly in hock to a pawnbroker whom

5. The name given locally to the small-loan racket where the operator lends five dollars until the next payday, without security, and receives six dollars in repayment.

6. This involves the time-purchase of a piece of expensive jewelry which is kept by the seller as security for the loan. The borrower pays two rates, one for the time payments, and a second for the loan proper. He never has possession of the article and is constantly faced with the possibility ˀf having his wages garnisheed if he misses a single payment.

they patronized frequently, although his shop was almost two miles distant.[7]

### Occupational and Employment Status:

The families varied widely in the occupations pursued by working members. Table V shows the wide range of the occupations of the fathers. Forty-three (69.5 percent) were classed as laborers, although their occupations often had more impressive titles. For example, the father in the Czabot family was known as a "custodian" in his place of employment although his actual work was that of an unskilled odd-job man or laborer.

TABLE V

*Occupations of the Heads of Families*

| Laborers | 43 | Upholsterer | 1 |
|---|---|---|---|
| Porters | 4 | Pastry cook | 1 |
| Chauffeurs | 2 | "Second man" (domestic) | 1 |
| Furniture movers | 2 | Meat handler | 1 |
| Elevator operators | 2 | Bus conductor | 1 |
| Die cutter | 1 | Grocery clerk | 1 |
| X-ray technician | 1 | Soft drink salesman | 1 |
| | | Total | 62 |

Six of the mothers were employed outside the home. One acted as janitress for the tenement house in which the family lived, two worked in a small factory as part-time packing clerks, and three had irregular employment as domestics in the middle-class and upper-class apartment areas a few blocks away.

Four families had young male members who worked outside the home, three of them as clerks, the fourth as a laborer. Only three families had older daughters who worked, two as part-time department store clerks, the other as a typist.

Unemployment had been experienced in the past, but during the period of the study only one case of unemployment was encountered, which will be discussed later.

7. This individual, known locally (and rather affectionately) as "the sheeney," has a large clientele among low-income families in Yorkville. He is patronized, even though at a distance, to avoid unfavorable publicity for the families locally. The business mores of this group prohibit any admitted use of a pawnbroker's services.

*Educational Status:*

The formal education of the adult members of these families varied largely in relation to the nativity of the individuals. Among the foreign-born, those with an agrarian background commonly had not more than four or five years of schooling, much of that under the guidance of the village priest. Among the few foreign-born of urban origin, the educational status was somewhat higher. The individuals in this group had gone to school, on the average, until they were from twelve to fourteen years of age.

The native-born adults had fared somewhat better. Completion of grammar school or its equivalent was usual, and almost half had had one or two years of high school. Seven had graduated from the New York City high schools.

Most of the foreign-born men had received some "Americanization" lessons from one source or another after arriving in New York. Only a few of the foreign-born women had had such training—whatever command of English and of American ways of life the latter had secured came from contacts with family members or through outside social affiliations.

*Religious Affiliations:*

Sixty-one percent of the families—thirty-eight of the sixty-two—were Catholics, with membership in one or another parish church in the vicinity of the block. Another twelve families (38 percent) identified themselves as Protestant, but only seven were affiliated with a church in the neighborhood. The remaining eleven of this group identified themselves as "belonging" to one or another denomination in the Protestant church, but were not active in any church organizations. The remaining six families were sure that they were not Catholics, but never were able to identify themselves definitely as anything else.

*Social Relationships:*

The families varied greatly in the kind, number, and degree of affiliations outside the home. All of the families, with two exceptions, had at least one other family with whom regular contacts were maintained—some had as many as ten. A few went no farther than across the street for their social visits—others journeyed to Queens or Astoria (outside the Borough of Manhattan) to keep up weekly visits which had originated when these particular friends were neighbors in earlier days.

These friendships uniformly had a patterned regularity. For example, "on Tuesday nights we always play euchre with the Garvot family, either here or at their house. Then on Friday nights we always go to the Willitz's (their flat is bigger than ours) where we play hearts with them and the Bruckner family." This routinism appears to stabilize the relationship, to give it a special quality not found in irregular visits, and to break the monotony and boredom of low-income life. This will be discussed in more detail in a later chapter.

Organizational affiliations were less uniformly entered into. Some families were very active in all types of organizations, and belonged to church, settlement, and political clubs. In some cases where the father was foreign-born, the family belonged to a Sokol or dancing club, or to informal clubs built around nationality interests. If the father was a member of a trade union, the family found some social outlets through union parties.

Mothers in this group rarely belonged to parent-teacher groups— foreign-born mothers with children in school ordinarily keep as far away from the school as possible. The younger mothers attended well-baby clinics—foreign-born mothers shunned, for the most part, any medical facilities until urgently needed.

The organization affiliations of these families were so closely related to the organization of the family as such that a more detailed discussion is left for a future chapter.

These, then, were the families with which this study was concerned in its search for the effects of trouble in the lives of the low-income urban dweller. In this group of families we have neither the worst of urban humanity, in a social sense, nor have we urban humanity at its best, in an economic sense. We do have something of a cross-section of the thousands of families living in the dozens of city blocks which make up the poorer areas of New York City's Middle East Side.

# CHAPTER THREE

# The Organization of These Families

IN CHAPTER ONE it was stated that the effects of troubles upon the family cannot be considered without a knowledge of the adequacy of the family's organization. The basic criteria for such adequacy were given as follows: (1) There must be a consciousness of and acceptance by each member of his own and of the complementary roles in the family; (2) family members must have a willingness to accept the common good of the family over their own good; (3) the family must provide satisfactions within the family unit; (4) the family must have a sense of direction and be moving in keeping with this, to however small a degree.

Families were expected to vary in the degree to which they met these criteria of adequacy. It is conceivable that in a sub-culture less complicated than the one under consideration families might be found which fitted all criteria amply. In a highly complex urban culture such as this, with its many and discordant demands, it would be a rare family indeed that could hold an optimum position in all of these criteria. The degree of adequacy of organization of families, in other words, cannot be attributed solely to the efforts of that family, but must be seen as something that is culturally conditioned and therefore symptomatic of the state of the culture.

From the earliest days of the field work it was evident that these families varied greatly in this respect. In a few of the families they were so obviously in accord, so smoothly functioning, as to raise no question concerning the adequacy of organization. In another few, the discords were so evident—so constant and intense—that there was no doubt of the inadequacy of their organization. In most of the families, however, the determination was not easy. Conflicts in various areas of family life were readily discerned in some families— and were found in others only after a considerable period of study. There are a number of these which contribute to the median position of the majority of the families, and they need to be discussed before any assignment of adequacy is given.

EARLIER TROUBLES AND INADEQUACY

Residuals of past troubles or crises were present in some families. For example, where death or chronic illness had caused a displacement of roles in recent months, families were found to be inadequately organized. This appeared to be in direct proportion to the recentness of the trouble. Conversely, the farther from the event, the more likely were the individuals in the family to have adjusted themselves to the new requirements of their roles.

In the Gregory family, where the oldest son assumed the major roles formerly held by the father (now chronically ill with arthritis), the family members had found it difficult to adjust to the new situation. There was an unwillingness on the part of the younger children to transfer their obedience to their oldest brother; due to the differential between the father's and son's wages there was a reduced family income, which (together with other factors) made it difficult for the mother to adjust to the son's new position; and the son experienced difficulty in assuming not only the breadwinner role but also complementary roles. The son's description of his position (given seven months after the trouble, the retirement of the father) relative to the new situation is enlightening.

> *Since pop got sick, I have had to bring all of the money to the family, and that hurts! But that isn't all. The real trouble is fitting into pop's shoes; the kids didn't see why I should be boss now that pop wasn't able to be around, and they wouldn't do what I had to tell them to do most of the time. Mom got fussed because I didn't*

*earn what pop had, and that made trouble because she didn't trust me to make decisions the way pop did. It gets better, though, as we go along. Maybe you don't know it, but this being a father in a family isn't easy. Maybe when you grow up to it, it's O.K., but to get a ready-made family isn't good.*

Where there had been no role substitutions but only role devaluations resulting from a trouble, the same relative condition was found, *i.e.*, the re-establishing of earlier role evaluations had not been completed.

In the Roberts family, where the father's earlier inadequate handling of the health problem had made him the butt of family ridicule with role devaluation, he had not been able to bring back his former role evaluation, and the family was still somewhat disorganized as a result.

*When I messed up things, our family all razzed me so that I couldn't have any control over the kids. My wife never did have any, at any time, and so we've been in a hell of a mess. The kids won't pay attention to me, and they won't pay attention to Gert, so they just run. It's a little better, though, lately. I guess they're forgetting or else I'm redeeming myself some way.*

### CONFLICTS AND INADEQUACY

Conflicts within the family also prevented many families from being considered adequately organized. These factors were in some instances culturally engendered; in others they were the result of personal difficulties. (It is impossible to establish a clear dichotomy between cultural and personal factors; their interdependence is too well-known to need elaboration here.) It is essential, however, that we indicate some of the areas in which the conflicts had developed for these families.

A major characteristic of the conflicts which appeared to be culturally engendered was that they involved directly the two generations of the family and therefore weakened its internal structure. These conflicts were as follows:

*Conflicts Due to Cultural Disparity:*

Conflicts between parents and children over standards in the home were found most often. Not only was this true of families with foreign-born parents; it was also true of native-born families whose incomes had held them to a low plane of living while the children were learning outside the home to expect a higher plane of living.

This type of conflict appeared, for both foreign-born and native-born families, when the children were in or approaching adolescence. At the time when children were ready to enter into family affairs in a more responsible and mature way, these conflicts defeated the contribution the children might have made because of their more extensive knowledge of urban resources and urban ways. The conflicts provided a wedge which drove the two generations apart and made the family less a "unity of interaction."

In the foreign-born families these conflicts were based not so much upon physical disparities in the homes as upon differences in the culture patterns.[1] Where the parents (or one parent) were living according to an old-world culture pattern, and the standards of family behavior were at variance with those of other homes the children considered "American," conflict resulted. In nineteen of the twenty-seven families with one or both parents foreign-born, these conflicts were present but varied in direct relation to the rigidity of the parental standards.

In the Knecht family, with the father and mother both German-born (Prussian), the parental concepts of the authoritarian and disciplinarian roles of the father (culturally determined) were divergent from those of the children, both of whom were in high school. As the children saw the freedom possessed by their friends, their own inability to be away from home in the evening, to choose their own companions, to wear clothes of their own choice—anything, in fact, which aided in creating a consciousness of social distance between

1. The Chapin Scale for Rating Living Room Equipment was applied to this group of homes. The range for the sixty-two homes was 24–86, with a mean rating of 46.4. For a random sample of low-income urban homes in this general area, 500 in number, the range was 20–90, with a mean rating of 44.2 (from an unpublished study by the writer).

these children and their associates—produced conflict. Gerhardt, the sixteen year-old son, described the conflict in these words:

*We don't get along so well in our family, it's because father and mother demand that we live the way they lived as children in their families in Kulm. But everyone we know, even in some German families, lives differently, and its hurts us and makes us—me especially—angry inside. So I fight back still more, and so it goes. I want to get away just as much as I can now, and I'll go away to live as soon as I have a job.*

The fact that many parents possessed sufficient insight to realize that they fought a rear-guard action in such matters, and submitted somewhat to the demands of their children, alleviated such effects in some families. One of the mothers made the following statement which typified the attitude of many parents:

*We don't like what our kids do always. But what can you do? The school teaches them things different from what we want, and they want to dress and do things the way they see others in their school do. Maybe it's all right, maybe we are the ones who are wrong. But we'd like to have our children be the way we want them to be.* All we can do, I guess, is give in when we have to, *and try to raise them the best we can.*

Similar conflicts were found in families which attempted to preserve the cultural heritage by adhering to old-world customs. In the Zarysk family, for example, the parents insisted that the children dress in Hungarian peasant costumes and join in adult parties which featured native dances. These attempts met with rejection (with good reason, as the children viewed the situation):

*Pop and mom always want to go to their parties and dance the old dances. Nuts! We'd look silly, wouldn't we? None of our friends do that sort of thing, and they only laugh at us if we do them. That's the trouble, you can't be like other kids and do what your parents want, too.*

In the native-born families, this type of conflict centered more upon the material standards of the home. With furniture and radios —everything, in fact, that is used in the home—changing style, the standards-conscious child wanted his or her home kept up to date, an impossibility for low-income families.

In the Beckett family (with total earnings of less than $25 for a family of five) the furniture was poor, both in quality and style, although kept scrupulously clean and in condition. The children played with others whose homes were equipped with the time-payment, blonde-mahogany-veneer-bright-colored-upholstery-garish-design furniture which is (apparently) standard for the "well-furnished" low-income home in urban centers. The obvious differences were productive of conflict; Mrs. Beckett described the situation as follows:

> *The children see all of these nice new things, furniture and all the rest, and then come home and nag for us to have things like them. Mary says she can't get a boy friend because we are laughed at for being behind the times. When the children talk about these things, it upsets the mister and then he gets mad at them and at me, and we have trouble. I try to keep the children from talking about how other people's tenements are fixed up, but I guess it's pretty hard not to see the difference.*

One of Mary's statements showed the children's attitude in this type of situation:

> *My family can't see what it does to us to have to live different from other families. Why, I brought a boy home and he saw how poor our house is, and he never came back, even when I asked him to. We can't have our friends come to our house, and then when we don't, they don't ask us to their house very often, so we lose our friends. If only we could make our father see how it does things to us, we'd get along better. He gets so mad at us that mother doesn't even want us to talk at home. What kind of a home is that?*

These, of course, are conflicts which are particularly important in a low-income urban group such as the one under study. The second generation lives under the handicap of having not only the between-cultures differences focused sharply for them, but also of having the additional problem of differences between levels in the culture well-defined.

### Conflicts Due to Religious Differences:

A second source of conflict, closely allied to the previous one, lay in differences in religious beliefs. Where parents adhered rigidly to religious beliefs or were meticulous in the observance of church rites, the children were frequently restive under their parents' attempts to dictate in such matters. With the present emphasis upon science and material values in our culture, this was not unexpected. Children in the upper grammar school and high school grades were constantly having new intellectual vistas opened to them—vistas different from the traditional teachings of the church, both Catholic and Protestant. A sixteen year-old Protestant boy verbalized the conflict in his family in these words:

> *My father and mother believe all that stuff about Adam and Eve. I know it isn't so, we learn about such things in biology. When I don't want to go to church and hear that same old stuff, they think I'm a heathen and raise the devil with me. So then I get mad, and I don't do anything they want me to.*

### Conflicts Arising from Adolescent Sex Behavior:

While occurring less frequently, a powerful source of disunity in these families was found in the differing sex mores of the parents and children. The parents made few efforts to teach their children even the rudiments of sex knowledge (and the schools did little more), but they showed a general concern about the sex habits of the younger generation.[2] Such concern, however, led only to in-

2. It should be mentioned here that, in the light of their own behavior norms, this concern was well-founded. Based upon several informal studies in this area, it is the writer's considered opinion that more than half of the children have engaged in sex practices before they reach the age of sixteen. The knowledge of contraceptives is widespread among children in this area—more so than among their parents—and contraceptive devices are easily obtained by children of all ages.

creased intra-family tension, and not to any activities designed to better existing conditions.

The Farber children were thought by their parents to be engaging in sex practices with school companions. Mrs. Farber had found contraceptive devices in the fifteen-year-old daughter's purse, and attempts to discipline the children included withholding pocket money and refusing new clothes for the daughter. Conflicts resulted, but neither parent made any real effort to give the children an understanding of their position regarding pre-marital sex relations. The seventeen-year-old son, in a long discussion with the writer, gave the following explanation of his and his sister's point of view:

> *Kids act like other kids, and my people don't understand that. Today there isn't anything wrong about screwing, all the kids in our school do it, and why not? Girls know how to be careful, and you can always get rubbers anywhere. If there was any chance of knocking a girl up, that would be different. But when my people grew up they had to take chances, so they didn't do it. Besides they didn't know as much as we do now. So they think we should be pure like they were. Can't you have any fun in life? Not according to them, you can't. And they're always saying that it's a sin. Jeez, even the priests don't give you so much hell about it anymore. . . . If you want to have a good time, and be like the other kids around, you just got to do some things they do, even if you didn't want to. But boy, there's sure hell in our house sometimes. When mom found the rubbers in Marie's pocketbook, why she was fit to be tied for a month, and so was pop. We didn't even get a decent meal thrown at us, and they just looked at us every time we came in. We sure didn't rate in our family for a while.*

*Conflicts Due to Uneven Assimilation:*

In the families with one or both parents foreign-born, another type of conflict arose as a result of the difference in the degree to which parents had become "American." Because the husbands made acquaintances and friends outside the home, and had more contacts through their workday world, the degree of assimilation was usually more marked in the husband than in the wife. This precipitated conflict between the two in some instances, but more significantly, it created conflict between the parents and the children. Not only did the children resent the inability or unwillingness of one parent to become "American," but further difficulty arose when one parent came to the defense of the other. The result was a three-way conflict.

In the Zingara family, the father had progressed much farther in his adoption of American ways than had his wife. In his work contacts he had come to accept new food patterns, standards of dress, the new language, etc., and took pride in his progress toward being an American. Mrs. Zingara, on the contrary, retained her old-country ways, and was strongly identified with other foreign-born Italian women in the area. Mr. Zingara was constantly irked by the contrast between his wife and other women in the block, and by her resistance to efforts on his part to Americanize her. She, in turn, was suspicious of her husband's new ways, and accused him frequently of going with other women. (All of this after twenty years in the United States.)

The Zingara children resented the mother's resistance to change, and were open in their criticism of her. This in turn brought the father to her defense, and sharp differences between the father and the children resulted. When these three-way conflicts reached their peak, which occurred at intervals, the four members of the family were consequently divided into three factions, each attempting to assert itself at the expense of the others.

The contributions which these types of conflict make should not be under-estimated, at least in this series of families. Wherever these conflicts were present in the family, the basic disunity which resulted prevented the family's presenting a solid front either to trouble or to the community when in trouble. Not only did role acceptances suffer, but the families also tended not to put the interests of the family first. Since family unity is not something that can be turned on or off at will, or brought into being only when needed, families with these underlying conflicts may be less well-equipped than those in which more personal types of conflict occur.

The more personal types of conflict, *i.e.*, those which appeared to have arisen out of psychological difficulties between individuals, and which may be called inter-personal, follow:

*Parent's Conflicts over Children:*

In many of the families there were conflicts which were due to differences between parents in matters of discipline, spending money, religious participation, and the like. In these families, the children accepted the demands of the parent, and adjusted to them, but the conflict between the parents continued in spite of this adjustment. No set patterns were found, each family seeming to have its own particular causes of the inter-parent strife. The following are examples of such conflicts.

In the Lehr family, where the father was a strict disciplinarian, the parents were in conflict. The mother attempted to shield the children from this severity, and in so doing, created constant tension between herself and her husband. As a result there were few times when the parents were able to face unusual situations in their lives without sharp insecurity and the need for new patterns of action.

In the Hammer family, the reverse was true. The mother tried to keep the children within the home, and to censor their choice of companions. The father interceded frequently in an effort to have the children widen their circle of friendships, and such intercession usually resulted in a period of tension. Mr. Hammer spoke of the situation in the following words:

> We get along all right in our family except that we're always on edge about the children. My wife wants to keep them at home, and not let them run with kids in the neighborhood she thinks are bad for them. It doesn't really hurt our family, it just keeps us keyed up all of the time. We'll never go to smash over it, but it would help if things weren't this way.

In the Clarke family the mother attempted to dictate the religious beliefs and observances of the children to an extreme degree. Mr. Clarke opposed such dictation, tried to help the children to think through their religious problems, and to ease the situation with their mother. As a result, the parents were always in a state of tension, and whole-hearted coöperation was lacking.

In two families the mother, realizing the children's need for money to meet school expenses, attempted to give them a small but regular allowance. In each case the father, who did not believe in letting children handle money until they were earning it, resented the mother's interference, and minor conflict persisted.

In two other families the mother, probably influenced by the drive by the Catholic League for Decency for cleaner movies, attempted to keep the children from attending the neighborhood movie houses, and met resistance from the father. In both families some tension resulted, especially when the mothers were particularly vocal about certain pictures.

These conflicts were rarely maintained at a high level, and most often ebbed and flowed as other conditions in the family's life changed. Despite the minor character of such conflicts, they were important in keeping the parents from the understanding and coöperation which are basic to well-organized family life.

*Conflicts Resulting from Sexual Maladjustment:*

There were several families in which poor sexual adjustment prevented an optimum of organization. The maladjustments in these families had either of two bases. In several families there was an obvious lack of understanding of techniques in the sex relationship, which resulted in a lack of satisfaction on the part of the wife and of discontent on the part of the husband. The resulting nervous tensions were sufficient to prevent the complete acceptance of their roles by either the wife or the husband.

In other families, the maladjustment resulted from a fear of pregnancy. This was indicated both in Catholic and Protestant families —in the former because of the Church's attitude toward birth control and because of ignorance—in the latter largely because of ignorance and superstition.[3] Since the fear of having too many and inadequately-spaced children was present in almost all of the women

3. The lack of accurate or adequate information concerning contraceptive measures was pronounced in this group of families. Only three of the families had had competent advice; seventeen used chemical or mechanical means of doubtful value; sixteen used the "free period" technique; twelve practiced withdrawal; the remaining fourteen no protection.

of child-bearing age, this effect upon the marital relationship was not unexpected.

In the Mifflin family, the wife had been badly frightened on her wedding night and had never recovered from that experience. Her husband was totally ignorant of the psychology of the sex act, spoke of "relieving" himself when he discussed intercourse, and resorted to prostitutes frequently after his failure to attain an adequate adjustment with his wife. This in turn only heightened the tensions created in the wife through inability to achieve satisfaction in her sex life.

In the Corbin family, where three children had been born in the first thirty-seven months of married life, Mrs. Corbin had been unable to accept her husband's advances for some years. He, in turn, had the traditional idea that his wife should submit to his advances at any time, and at the same time was unwilling to violate the religious sanctions against the use of contraceptives. The resulting tensions caused a considerable degree of conflict between the two.

*Conflict over Attachment to an Earlier Generation:*

The presence in the family of a member of an earlier generation, or the proximity of such in the neighborhood, was in several instances a cause of conflict between parents. In each instance the other parent felt that he or she was having to compete for emotional security and love. The attitude of one husband, Mr. O'Hara, was typical of such situations:

> *I think we'd get along better if it wasn't for her family. But they don't want to let her get away from them, and she's always running home to them instead of coming to me. Why, they even knew she was with child before I did. Then she thinks I am unfair when I get mad about it. I think she should have gotten rid of them when she married me—I mean, she should have become part of our family, not stayed with her, own.*

*Conflicts over the Economic Status of the Family:*

Conflict between the husband and wife centered upon the economic status of the family in several cases. In two of these, both husband and wife were foreign-born, and had looked upon their migration to America as an opportunity for bettering themselves economically and socially. When the bright hopes did not materialize, both of the husbands accepted their unexpected status and attempted to make the best of it. For the most part the wives followed suit, but there remained some dissatisfaction which was demonstrated occasionally.

Mrs. Gertman showed this in the following quotation, the substance of which she repeated at frequent intervals:

*The thing that makes me so mad is how John just lies down and lets the world walk over him. When we came [to the United States] he was going to be so much—we would get somewhere. Now look at where we are, at this tenement. I try to stand it most of the time, but I get mad because he won't get ahead, and then I boil over and spoil things.*

Her husband, in reviewing one of these periods of tension, which were frequent enough to keep the family in a state of unrest, offered the following explanation:

*Caroline is a good wife, but she gets disappointed with me because I'm just about where I was when we came to America. We came right after we got married so we could better ourselves. Well, things don't always work out the way you think they are going to. America takes more education to get along than I had. We had some sickness and got behind (and on wages like mine you never catch up), the depression made us take relief, so you are just where you started from. Women don't understand such big things, and she gets mad because she says I won't get ahead like I said I would. You just can't get ahead in a place like this—it's too big a problem.*

A third family, the Mangini's, was subject to conflict between the parents because Mr. Mangini would not try for a civil service position. To his wife, such a position—with its tenure, retirement pay, and other advantages (not excluding the social status which went with the job)—was desirable above all else, and she clothed such a position with a respectability which such positions rarely deserve.

To Mr. Mangini, who knew his limitations rather well, her urgings were a constant source of irritation, and produced between them an undertone of conflict.

*Conflicts over the Social Life of the Family:*

Another source of conflict between the parents was that resulting from the wife's social activities and demands. In some families the wives attempted to carry on social activities which were not acceptable to their husbands, either for financial reasons or from lack of interest. This type of conflict was found in the younger families, where the social activities of courtship days had not yet been supplanted by the more somber patterns of low-income family existence. An example is found in the Sylvester family, where the husband characterized his situation in the following words:

> *Jeez, I love my wife and all that stuff, but she can't seem to learn we're married now. I know we used to go all the time before we married, at least, as much as I had money for, but hell, we're married now and got Julia [the two year-old daughter] and we can't afford this go-go-go stuff. Besides, she doesn't seem to know you have to quiet down as you get older.*

*Conflict over the Handling of Money:*

In many families there were conflict situations involving the handling of the family finances. Inability to distribute the amount available for food over the whole period from one payday to the next was a frequent source of irritation. In the Kitler family, both husband and wife realized this, but with different reactions:

> *She's a good cook and housekeeper, but she bothers me like hell the way she handles money. I get paid on Friday: we eat good every Saturday but by the middle of the next week we're down to poor eating, and maybe we have only eggs or not even that by the next Friday. She would be an A-1 wife if it wasn't for that.*

Mrs. Kitler's attitude was somewhat different from that of her husband, and is quoted because it demonstrates the lack of acceptance of complementary roles.

*I know he gets mad at me about my managing. I want to feed him and the kids right—he likes his food so much—and I mean to feed him right all of the time. Only it's hard to make the money last. Things look so good in the store when I have the money and so I buy them, and then he doesn't think I should have. If he'd help me to save the money for the week . . . , but he says it's my job and that it's my fault and he won't help me.*

In other families, the reverse of this was true. In the Farnham family, the husband kept a tight control of the family purse, and doled out small sums daily for the household purchases. Mrs. Farnham was better able to manage than was her husband, but had never been able to convince him of that fact. The result was a constant conflict which never became a serious threat only because of adequacy in other areas of family life.

These conflicts had a dual importance in the lives of these families. They affected, first of all, the adequacy of the family organization in terms of the first three criteria employed. Failure to measure up to the fourth criterion, *i.e.*, having a sense of direction and be moving in keeping with it to however small a degree, was a condition found in many of the families. It appears that this low-income group, lacking money with which to do and about which to plan, was less sensitive to long-time desires and less susceptible to "the golden promises of the future" than are the middle- and upper-class families. While this criterion cannot be considered as having the importance of the other three, it is still important enough to be used in considering the degree of family adequacy.

Beyond this immediate effect upon the adequacy, however, is the long-time attenuating influence of such conflicts. Many of these families had begun with full promise of being successful within the cultural and economic limits of their environment, only to have their family structures gradually eroded by the presence of these conflicts. It is this continuing effect which weakens many families and makes them more vulnerable to trouble than would be the case were they free from such conflicts.

THE PATTERN OF DOMINANCE

In none of these families was there any real balance of power between husband and wife. The basic pattern, in all of the families, was patriarchal.[4] The husband was the provider—the wife the homemaker and rearer of the children; the personality, will, and interests of the husband were dominant over those of other members of the family. Surrogateships might be established, if necessity demanded —the wife did go out to work in a number of families, for example— but the husband remained the provider and *head* of the family. This pattern of dominance was found to be affected greatly by troubles, however, and needs to be kept in mind.[5]

NARCOTIZATION

Two of the families were so strikingly different in their reactions to the study and to the interviewer that special attention should be paid them. At the first interview, in both families, the condition of the physical equipment of the home, the lack of cleanliness and order, and the general apathy of the respondents marked them as differing from the general run of families in the block. The greatest differences, however, were not in the physical condition but in the psychological and social attitudes of the family members. The psychiatric term "loss of affect" (loss of feeling, emotion, and desire as determining factors in an individual's conduct) could well be applied to all of the members of the two families. There was, however, not only a loss of affect on the individual level but an accompanying loss of interaction as a family. There was no apparent sense of interdependence, except in matters of physical well-being, and here it was low.

The best interviewing techniques the writer was able to marshal

4. The patriarchal pattern evolved from one of three basic causes: (1) It was institutionally set, as in the case of most of the foreign-born or second-generation families; (2) it was determined by husband-wife relationships, *i.e.*, the wife's love for or psychological need of the husband permitted or demanded such a pattern; (3) it was determined by dominance of personality, economic dependence, or physical coercion.

5. *Cf.* the discussion of changes in the dominance pattern in Chapter Six.

failed to strike any responsive chord; at the same time there was no antagonism on the part of the family—only an acquiescence that was completely neutral in tone. Had this phenomenon not been of interest to the investigator, these families would have been rejected at the end of the first interview. Both families discussed their difficulties, both past and present, with frankness, *and with no apparent feeling about them.* Both had had unemployment, death, and disorganization due to other troubles, but now appeared to be unconcerned about them. All in all, the attitude of each was an apathy toward the world about it.

There were several distinctive features in both families which should be mentioned:

The family existence in the earlier years had been according to the usual urban, low-income pattern (with the usual friendships, memberships in organizations, etc.). Both families had now withdrawn completely from such relationships, both formal and informal. Both families had suffered a series of crises, not necessarily related but occurring in rapid succession. Both had suffered prolonged unemployment and the experience of being dependent upon public relief for an extended period, in both instances because of generalized unemployment rather than personal failure.

The father in one of the adequately organized families had known the first of these narcotized families for many years, and had been very friendly with them until a few years ago. His account of the deterioration of the family is of interest:

> *They used to be just like anybody else. They had friends. We went there a lot and they visited us, and belonged to the same Sokol we did. John was doing all right—didn't have any more than we did, but was getting ahead. Now that is all changed. She got sick first, when she was with her second child, and finally lost it. John did all the housework for almost two years while he worked days. Then he lost his job, just before the depression and couldn't seem to be able to get another one. It's funny, the way that family changed. She was a good housekeeper, now she doesn't care any more. Just does what she has to do. He has a job now that the*

*welfare got him or he'd never worked again, probably. They stopped going to the Sokol and to Jan Hus—they didn't seem to want to see their friends at all anymore—the punch is all gone out of life for all of them. It's got the boy, too, now—he doesn't do anything but hang around. We don't see them anymore, because they don't want us. When we did see them, at the last, they just acted like they didn't have any feeling for each other at all.*

The condition in these families was extreme, of course. It raises the question, however, of whether or not families which are subject to repeated troubles and which are less adequately organized may suffer some degree of narcotization.

### COMPENSATIONS FOR CONFLICTS

Establishing the degree of adequacy of organization in any one family as compared with the others in the group was of course highly subjective. It was not made easier by the fact that where there were inadequacies of adjustment in one phase of life there were sometimes compensating superior adjustments in other phases. The following are examples of these compensations:

In the Taylor family, where there was constant strife over the way in which money was handled by the father, the very adequate sexual adjustment of the parents tended to keep the family on an even keel. Mrs. Taylor explained the situation in these words:

*I get SO DAMNED MAD at the Mister because of the way he wastes money. He doesn't have any sense at all where a dollar is concerned—buys the kids anything crazy he sees and thinks they'd like. Then when he's with me [in the sexual relationship] I forget all of that and forgive him his weakness. It it wasn't for that, I'd of left him long ago.*

In the Richmond family, where there was a lack of adjustment at intervals because of the wife's extreme ambition for social position, the conscientious way in which she cared for the baby acted as a compensating factor for the father who was exceptionally fond of children.

In the Derber family, where there were tensions because of religious differences, compensations resulted from the high degree of sexual adjustment, which (as in the Taylor family above) tended to attenuate the difficulties of family adjustment.

After the histories of all the families had been compiled and the family interaction observed for several weeks, each family was considered in the light of the criteria employed, the conflicts and compensations were evaluated, and the families were then ranked as accurately as possible for their relative adequacy of organization. This was an internal evaluation, that is, not against any normative family in the culture. It is obvious that such a ranking was difficult, subject to personal interpretation and possible bias on the part of the investigator, and, to say the least, empiric. Such a ranking was necessary, however, if the relation of family organization to performance in trouble was to be understood.[6]

After ranking, the families were divided into three categories: *better-than-average*, *average*, and *below-average*. These three categories will be employed, under these same names, in the later discussions.

Excluding the two families described above as being narcotized, the sixty remaining families in the study were grouped as follows: twelve were *better-than-average*, thirty-four were *average*, and fourteen were *below-average*. The characteristics of the three groups need be reviewed only briefly here.

The twelve families with *better-than-average* organization had a high degree of role acceptance, both personal and complementary. There was a strong sense of the common good, with an accompanying sense of direction in which the family moved. Uniformly these families provided normal satisfactions within the family group. The Harper family is an example in this group:

Both Mr. and Mrs. Harper were born in New York City, Mr. Harper within six blocks of where the family now lives. Mr. Harper graduated from high school, Mrs. Harper quit high school after the third year. They were married when they were 23 and 21 respectively,

6. *Cf.* Chapter One.

and lived with Mr. Harper's parents a year while getting together furniture for their own home. Mr. Harper has worked for the same company as a janitor for the last twenty-one years (since he was twenty-eight years of age), and has never earned more than $34.50 per week, his present wage.

There are three children; Michael, born in 1927; Mary, born in 1929; and Virginia, born in 1931. The first child was not born until eight years after the marriage—"we wanted to try to have a little money saved up before we had any children." The Harpers planned for three children—"that's all we think we can bring up in this world." Michael will graduate from high school this year; the two girls are both in their proper grades in school and making adequate records.

In the home Mr. Harper is the dominant person. He is recognized as "the boss," both by virtue of his being the father in the family and because all of the members love and respect him. There is no bossiness in his manner, however; he defers to Mrs. Harper and the children in conversations, and says that "Mother really runs the house." There is a clear-cut understanding in the family that each member has certain responsibilities and that he or she assumes those responsibilities. There is no compulsion in this—"that's the way our family works. Each one knows his rights and his duties and expects to do both."

The five members of the family belong to the Lutheran Church on —— St., and their intellectual and social interests are met through the activities of that church. There are six families with whom the Harpers are friendly; all six are also members of the church.

The family thinks of itself as a unit, and there is the subjugating of personal desires where the family good is concerned. "We've always taught the children that they had to let things they wanted go if it interfered with what the family had to have." The family discusses its major objectives and needs, and the children have always been encouraged to state their needs and have been helped to understand why other needs came first.

The parents have always tried to make the flat a center for the children's activities. "We've always wanted them to feel that here they could find what they needed, a place to bring their friends, things to do,—we didn't ever want our children to *have* to go to a neighbor's or to anybody else for what they wanted to do."

The Harper family has three objectives: getting Michael through high school and one of the city's colleges, toward which they have been saving small amounts for years, and giving each daughter enough training (outside of high school) in home-making so that she will be able to establish a good home. "We can't send all three to college, but we can teach the girls how to have a good home so they can marry a nice boy and have a family." Each girl has a bride's chest full of hand-worked linens made by herself under the mother's guidance, and each girl has been trained thoroughly in cooking and buying for the family.

Even with this brief description it should be evident that this family was adequately organized. There was great family solidarity, with recognition of the individual's roles and rights. The family had a strong sense of common good, and definite goals toward which it worked. It is apparent, even at a casual glance, that the Harper family was a closely-knit social unit.

The fourteen families classed as *below-average* were conspicuous in their uniformly *not* having an adequate role consciousness, either personal or complementary; in having no common family good which involved the subordination of personal aims, and in having the kind of home life which provided few or no satisfactions for the individual members. Outstanding in this group was the lack of a sense of direction and of movement in that direction. The Vogel family is neither the best nor the worst of this group, but illustrates the reasons for assigning it to the *below-average* group.

Mr. Vogel was born in Prussia, Mrs. Vogel in Bavaria. They met on board ship on the way to America, and Mr. Vogel persuaded her to marry him as soon as they had been cleared through Ellis Island. They were both 26 years of age when they married, and he was the first man who had ever paid any serious attention to her. Neither parent had completed grammar school before coming to America, but both took some "Americanization lessons" after arriving.

There were two children: Mina, born in 1932, and Karl, born in 1933. Mr. Vogel did not want any children, and both "came because of carelessness." He had never been interested in the home, even in the first years of married life, and had always spent a good part of his time in a Prussian drinking club in upper Yorkville. He had "always harbored bitterness in his heart because he wasn't born good enough to be an army officer." After the second child was born, Mr. Vogel lost his remaining interest in Mrs. Vogel, and treated her "like a hired maid." "I'm just here to take care of his house and his children, he thinks."

Mr. Vogel is a chauffeur for a family on Madison Avenue; in his wife's words, "he works steady and likes his job because it has a nice uniform in it—all Prussians are like that." He earns $30 a week, plus his uniforms and meals, but Mrs. Vogel never sees but one dollar a week of that. On Mondays (his day off from his job), he goes with her to the stores and buys everything for the week except milk and bread. Mrs. Vogel and the children are subject to his decisions as to clothes and their personal lives. "Karl hates his father because he will never let him do anything, but he isn't old enough yet to do anything about it." The family belongs to no church, and Mrs. Vogel belongs only to a card club. "They never meet in our place: everybody knows how the Mister feels about it."

Mrs. Vogel believes that the children should have an adequate home life, but sees no way of giving it to them as long as she has no money, and as long as every move she and the children make is dictated by her husband. "Karl is growing away from home already, and I can't do anything about it. He hangs around with that gang downstairs, and when I say anything his father only laughs at me."

In this family there are no plans for the future. Mr. Vogel keeps his own counsel, but Mrs. Vogel thinks he spends all of his money on drinking. "I know he goes with women some times, too, and that must cost him a lot of money. There isn't anything for me to plan ahead toward, anyway. I'd leave if I could, but this is the only way

I can be sure Mina and Karl and I will have even this much of a home."

While there was a consciousness of *his* role on the part of the father in this Vogel family, it is quite obvious that there was no sharing, no acceptance of complementary roles in the family. There was no common good toward which this family moved, and no family solidarity, even between the children and their mother. The Vogel family was definitely not a closely-knit social unit, and is obviously *below-average*.

The *average* group, less easy to characterize, varied from family to family. In some the conflicts discussed earlier in this chapter were of sufficient degree to be a source of inadequacy, but were compensated for by an exceptional adjustment in another area of family life. In others, the conflicts were only minor irritations, but sufficient to make difficult the role acceptances. In still others, the family lacked adequacy because the role structure was adequate but the home lacked the means for providing satisfactions within the home, a lack which served to ineffectuate the adequacy of the role structure.

The treatment of the troubles experienced, the solutions found or not found, and the intra- and inter-family effects of trouble are all to be considered in terms of these three broad groupings in the coming chapters.

# CHAPTER FOUR

# The Troubles of These Families

HAVING distinguished between exigencies and troubles, and having classified the families as to the adequacy of their organization, we turn now to the actual troubles which these families had during the study.

## THE OCCURRENCE OF TROUBLES

All of these families had had exigencies, but not all had had troubles. Table VI indicates the numbers of families [1] which had had troubles either prior to or during the study. The size of the group studied and the brief period of study make generalizations unwise, but there is immediately apparent a relation between the adequacy of family organization and the occurrence of trouble. While there are variations within categories—for example, the *better-than-average* group includes three families with troubles before the study but with none observed during the study, and four with no reported trouble prior to the study but with one or more troubles observed in the study period—there is an inverse relation between troubles and the adequacy of organization. This is especially apparent in the fourteen *below-average* families, all of which reported troubles prior to the study and had troubles while under observation.

This relation is further indicated in Table VII which shows the

1. The two families described in Chapter Three as *narcotized* were kept under observation but are not included in the following discussion.

TABLE VI

Distribution of Sixty Families by Non-trouble and Trouble Prior to and
During the Study, by Type of Family Adjustment

| | Number of families by type of adjustment | | |
|---|---|---|---|
| | Better-than-average | Average | Below-average |
| No troubles either prior to or during 24 months of study | 5 | — | — |
| No troubles prior to but one or more troubles during 24 months of study | 4 | 3 | — |
| One or more troubles prior to but no troubles during 24 months of study | 3 | 6 | — |
| One or more troubles prior to and one or more troubles during 24 months of study | — | 25 | 14 |
| Totals | 12 | 34 | 14 |

TABLE VII

Distribution of Sixty Families by Number of Troubles Experienced in
Study Period, by Type of Family Adjustment

| Number of troubles | Better-than-average | Average | Below-average |
|---|---|---|---|
| None observed | 8 | 6 | — |
| One | 3 | 1 | 1 |
| Two | 1 | 21 | 3 |
| Three | — | 5 | 6 |
| Four | — | 1 | 3 |
| Five | — | — | 1 |
| Total Families | 12 | 34 | 14 |

number of troubles experienced by the families in the two-year period. Two-thirds of the *better-than-average* families had no troubles, while less than one-fifth of the *average* and none of the *below-average* families were in this category. Conversely, none of the *better-than-average* families had three or more troubles, while six of the thirty-four *average* and ten of the *below-average* families had this number of troubles. This supports the earlier premise that adequacy of family organization is related to the family's trouble experience.

Since nearly one-fourth (fourteen) of these families had no troubles during the study, a first interest is in reasons for this freedom. What is it that makes a family trouble-proof?

The five families which reported no troubles prior to the study and in which no troubles were observed during the study were, first of all, outstanding in their possession of a strong role structure, with equally strong acceptance by the family members. The importance of role recognition and acceptance cannot be over-estimated. It was this quality which gave to these five families the unity which in turn served as a buffer against events that could easily change from exigencies into troubles. There was recognition by all five of the value to the family of knowing what each had to do in the way of contributing to family life. The father in the Keen family spoke of this fact in these words:

> One thing we've always tried to do in our family was to see that each one knew his place and knew what we expected of everybody else. It's hard to live the way we have to, but if everybody has a job in the family and does it, we get along all right. Our kids know that I earn the money, that Mother spends it, and that they have some responsibilities along that line, and believe me, that's what makes our family tick. Why, even in the depression when I didn't always earn enough to live on, we made out because we all knew what the problem was I faced, and we all tried to meet our own share in it.

Closely associated with this characteristic was the acceptance of a common definition of the good of the family. This meant, in practice, that the family thought of itself as a unit *and acted as a unit.* Nor was compulsion the motivating force in this unified action. This was well illustrated in the Wiltman family, where the mother told of the family unity in these words:

> *I guess one reason why we never had any trouble in our family is because we always pulled together. When we got married (that was in 1925 and times were good for us) we each knew that we had a job to do to make our family go, and we did it the best we could. We always tried to make the children see that that was the best way, by pulling together. When anything goes wrong, like it's sure to sometimes, we all pull in our belts and try to share the bad with the sweet. It isn't easy, sometimes it's real hard, but when you think that everybody in our family has his place and shares with everybody else, we go along together. And, you know, it works! Why even in depression times we weren't hurt bad. We took it in our stride, because it was our family together, and we're better for it now that times are good again. Our children understood what the family had to face, and each played his part.*

That this recognition of the effectiveness of the drive for a common good in the family is not confined to adults is shown by a statement of the seventeen year-old boy in this same family:

> *One place my family is sure different from some of my friends' is the way we all want the same things! I think Mom and Pop always want what's good for us as a family, and I know Sis and I do, too. We always work together, and if I can't have something because the family needs something else more, that's o.k., Mom has taught us why. Gee, when I have a family I sure want it to be that way.*

The third important characteristics of these five families was the effort by the family to provide for its members' interests within the home. Admittedly, in the complexities of the culture, these low-income families could not provide for all such satisfactions, but where surrogates were established *they were regarded as extensions of the home and not as substitutes for the home.* In the Schneider family, for example, the thirteen-year-old son was a member of the Boy Scout troop in a Protestant church in which the family held active membership. The family considered this troop membership not as a substitute for family life *but as an extension of it,* and made every effort to bring the boy's extra-mural scouting activities into the home. Mr. Schneider explained the relationship as follows:

> *We want John to go to his Scout meetings. We think he gets things there we can't give him in our home because of how we live. But we don't do it to get rid of him or to let him get away from us. His mother has his patrol group come here sometimes for a lunch, and I try to help him with his knots and to hear his badge lessons. . . . That's what a family's for: to help its children to meet their problems inside the family.*

Lack of space prevents the inclusion of other examples, but these families were uniform in their consolidation of interests within the home circle.

All of these families also had goals toward which they moved. Planning for the future, even though on a very small scale, appeared to be a definite, cohesive force in the family life. The objectives varied—putting the boy through college, owning a small home outside the city, moving to a newer part of the city,—but in each family there was such an objective, and it was recognized by all the members and all members shared in the effort to gain it.

It is of interest to note that socio-economic or educational status was not a determining factor in the adequacy of these families. Only one of the five was among those most comfortably situated by local standards. Two of them lived in the least desirable tenements in the block and had less than average incomes.

Before the remaining fifty-five families can be discussed, the types of troubles must be considered briefly. They fall logically into two groups, those not directly attributable to individual or family failure, and those which have this element. The first type includes troubles resulting from the depression, *i.e.,* unemployment due to lay-offs rather than to personal failure of the worker; to death and to illness, neither of which were directly attributable to personal failure. Quite different were the causes of trouble in the second group. Here aberrations in the personality of one or more members of the family, distortions in the role pattern for one reason or another, or the disturbance of social relations outside the family were the cause of the trouble. This second group result from defective handling of situations by the individuals involved, while the former group result from conditions beyond the control of the families.

The nine families (three *better-than-average* and six *average*) which reported troubles prior to the study but for which none were observed during the study pose certain questions at this point. Did these families learn from earlier troubles to avoid them during the study period? If so, what was learned? Also, were the earlier troubles of such a nature that they could not have been avoided?

The causes of the earlier troubles in these nine families were: Unemployment in depression years, five; Death in family, three; Illness in family, one; Failure of family to adjust to role changes, one; or a total of ten. (One *better-than-average* family in this group had had both unemployment and death as separate causes of trouble in the pre-study period.) It is noteworthy that with one exception (and that an *average* family) the causes of these troubles were not due to personal failure.

Just why these six *average* families experienced troubles before the study (with only one of these directly attributable to family failure) and experienced none during the study period cannot be answered except by speculation. There is an element of chance in all family life, of course, and it is certain to operate, of course, for these families.

But did families learn from earlier troubles to avoid further trouble? There are too few such events here on which to base any conclusions regarding this point, but the experience of the Berger family indicates that some families, at least, did benefit from earlier troubles. Mr. Berger's answer to this question gives some indication of what can happen.

*I don't think you learn very much from bein' in a jamb. The trouble is, if everything always happened the same, why you'd know what to expect. Now take me for instance: we never had any trouble in our family until five years ago when we had a sickness that damn near ruined us. Well, we got out of that mess all right, and now look at what happened just now when we lost the girl. The whole thing is, you never get in the same jamb twice—it just happens that you get a shot of bad luck and something goes wrong. There just ain't no map of the kind of jamb you're goin' to get into. The only thing that happens is you get kicked a little bit further down when somethin' happens, but you sure don't learn much!*

If Mr. Berger's opinion is at all typical, the families with few troubles do not learn much from experiencing troubles, probably because the initiating cause is different in each instance. It will be seen below that in the families with more frequent troubles, there are "repeaters" and families with distinct patterns of troubles.

### FAMILIES WITH TROUBLES

The types of troubles observed in these families are shown in Table VIII. These are listed as initiating causes although it was difficult in many instances to determine the primary cause. For example, where there was a violation by the child of the moral standards of the family (Czabot) and at the same time a health problem (the gonorrheal infection) as well as a problem of parent-child relationships, it was difficult to designate one as *the* initiating cause. Where this occurred, the one was designated as primary which was first to put in its appearance (in the Czabot family the health problem, without which the other problems would not have arisen).

The initiating causes divide into two types, financial and interpersonal. It should be kept in mind that the first type of troubles was concerned with financial problems *per se*, that is, the necessity for meeting financial obligations which resulted from death, illness, poor management or unemployment. The second type arose from the inability of the family to adjust to a particular situation within the family unit, such as illness, pregnancy, husband-wife conflict, and so on.

The significance of the distribution of these one hundred and

TABLE VIII

*Initiating Cause of 109 Troubles Observed During Study Period in 46 Families,
by Type of Adjustment*

| | | Type of Adjustment | | |
| | Total | Better-than-average | Average | Below-average |
|---|---|---|---|---|
| Financial problem resulting from: | | | | |
| Death | 8 | 3 | 4 | 1 |
| Illness | 15 | 1 | 10 | 4 |
| Poor Management | 12 | — | 9 | 3 |
| Unemployment | 1 | — | 1 | — |
| Inter-personal problem resulting from: | | | | |
| Acute illness | 26 | 1 | 14 | 11 |
| Chronic illness | 5 | — | 4 | 1 |
| Mental illness | 1 | — | 1 | — |
| Alcoholism | 1 | — | — | 1 |
| Pregnancy (legitimate) | 4 | — | 2 | 2 |
| Pregnancy (illegitimate) | 1 | — | 1 | — |
| Husband-wife conflict | 7 | — | 2 | 5 |
| Parent-child conflict | 6 | — | 2 | 4 |
| Sexual incompatibility | 7 | — | 3 | 4 |
| Death in family | 1 | — | 1 | — |
| Addition of grandparent to family | 1 | — | 1 | — |
| Indebtedness | 6 | — | 2 | 4 |
| Conflict with neighbors | 3 | — | — | 3 |
| Educational problem | 2 | — | 1 | 1 |
| International situation | 2 | — | 1 | — |
| Totals | 109 | 5 | 62 | 42 |

nine troubles experienced by the forty-six families is immediately apparent. Despite the small number of families, it appears that the less adequate the organization of the family the more frequent and important are the inter-personal problems as causes of trouble.

An important question at this point is whether or not there was a relation between the initiating causes of past troubles and those observed during the study period. Did the same causes recur, or were troubles set in motion each time by different causes? Among the thirty-nine families with troubles both before and during the study, was there any great number of families for whom the same troubles recurred? Twenty-two had the same initiating cause for successive troubles. These causes, with their frequencies, are as follows:

| | |
|---|---|
| Financial problem due to poor management | 5 |
| Inter-personal problem due to: | |
| Acute illness | 3 |
| Mental illness | 1 |
| Husband-wife conflict | 5 |
| Parent-child conflict | 4 |
| Sexual incompatibility | 2 |
| Indebtedness | 1 |
| Conflict with neighbors | 1 |
| Total | 22 |

Analysis of the case histories shows that many of these families were repeaters. For example, the Corbin family had not only been in conflict with neighbors in the last previous trouble, but had the same type of trouble with neighbors three times during the study (despite the fact that they moved once during the two years). Similarly, the McGuire family admitted poor management to have been the initiating cause in the last previous trouble, and experienced three troubles from the same cause during the study.

THE TROUBLES

In order to understand the reactions to troubles each of the initiating causes needs to be discussed in more detail.

*Financial Problems:*

It should be obvious that the lack of money is a basic cause of trouble in many low-income families. In this series, thirty-six of the troubles experienced were primarily due to the lack of money with which to meet needs, and another six resulted from the psychological effects of debt. It will shortly be seen that these are not one and the same.

(a) Resulting from death

Some students of family life apparently look with favor upon the psychological aspects of modern funeral practices.[2] The economic

2. *Cf.*, for example, Thomas Eliot's discussion of "Family Crises and Ways of Meeting Them" in H. Becker and R. Hill, *Marriage and the Family* (D. C. Heath and Co., Boston, 1942). Ch. XXII.

and social aspects were, for these families, hardly beneficial. It is no new discovery that funeral costs for any group are too high.[3] It was, in these eight families, this high cost which precipitated the trouble, despite the fact that they rode out the storm of bereavement.[4] The problem was one of being plunged into debt because of the necessity for providing a "good" funeral.[5]

The experience of the Wilbur family (*average*) was not atypical, and illustrates the kind of troubles into which families are plunged in this connection.

Mrs. Wilbur's mother, who had lived alone in a furnished room in the next block, died in January, 1942. She had reserves of less than seventy-five dollars. Mr. and Mrs. Wilbur, with a family income of thirty-two dollars per week and two children to support, felt the responsibility for the burial. Mrs. Wilbur's story of making the arrangements follows:

> *Not since we were married did we have anything to do with a funeral parlor. We didn't know where to go, but Harry said there is one on —— Street, so we went there. We didn't know the man, we just went in. We thought we could use mother's money, and make up the rest ourselves. On the way over, Harry said, "If we can pay seventy-five dollars cash, maybe he'll trust us for the other fifty or so."* . . . *Well, the man was very nice and said it was too bad mother died. He was real nice to us. Then he began to talk about what we'd want for a funeral, and said he'd do the best he could for us as far as money went, and we shouldn't worry a bit.*

3. Cf., for example, John C. Gebhart, *Report of the Advisory Committee on Burial Survey* (New York: Metropolitan Life Insurance Company, 1928).

4. This is not to say that death in the families did not concern these families. It happened that in only one was there "trouble" (in the sense used in this study) of an inter-personal nature.

5. The average cost of a funeral, to these eight families, was three hundred and sixty dollars, the range from two hundred and eighty dollars to four hundred and fifty dollars. Part of this cost is due to the high mark-up, part to the small and uneconomic size of the retailing unit, and no small part to the adding of unnecessary but "highly desirable" elements of service. On the basis of personal inquiry, the writer believes the adding of "highly desirable" elements of service to be most important. When approached for hypothetical service, most of the undertakers in this area stressed *"the things your mother would want if she were here to choose,"* and strong pressures were brought to bear to get the "nice" (and extra-cost) services into the contract.

*Then he showed us the boxes, and you know, he didn't have one for less than two hundred and fifty dollars, but of course that includes everything—his time and all, even the grave yard. I was upset, of course—I knew mother would die soon, but you're never quite ready for death, are you? Well, Harry wanted to do what I wanted, and the man talked so nice, we said after a while that we'd take the one at two hundred and eighty dollars. That wasn't the cheapest, but as the man said, we didn't want mother to have the cheapest thing. And we didn't. You love your dear ones, so you want to show your love for them, as he said. He admitted that we could get cheaper funerals some other places, but told us about how they treated the bodies. Besides, he said we could pay him fifty dollars down and five dollars a week without any interest. So we did—we signed a paper, and everything was done all right, it was a nice funeral. Small, just the family, but it was nice, the way mother would have wanted it.*

There was no reaction to the death or the funeral in this family. The "trouble" began three weeks later when the family felt the pinch of the five dollar weekly payment. Mr. Wilbur's statement follows:

*It was three weeks before we really saw the fix we were in! We'd always just got along on my pay, and now all of a sudden it was just like getting a pay cut of five dollars a week. Instead of having the usual worries of having just enough to go around as long as nothing else happened, we had this worry of not having enough to go around. We didn't know what to do. Then, last week I missed a day—you know that cold I had—and it meant I lost that extra amount. I didn't go in to pay him last Saturday, and Monday evening he sent somebody for the money. I said I didn't have it, that I'd been sick, and he said he'd show me what I signed.*

*Well, in the hurry of getting my wife's mother buried (you can't wait, you know), I guess I signed more than I knew I had. In the fine print at the bottom of the page (I hadn't read it) it said that I gave permission to have them take it out of my pay if I missed a week. "Garnish it," he called it. So what can I do? I know my boss might even fire me if they go to him. I can't lose my job. We'll just have to pay it, and not do something else we just have to do. How I can get along with this mess, I don't know! You know, there isn't any place we could have gone to keep out of this mess, even if we did see it coming!*

These two quotations indicate with sufficient clarity the way in which trouble arises out of a death. For the most part death was accepted as inevitable, and met adequately. The troubles in this family illustrate how the already present insecurity of low-income urban living is heightened and sharpened, and the usual patterns of action are blocked by the financial consequences of death.

(b) Resulting from illness

As the initiating cause of a financial problem, illness occurred fifteen times. In each instance the focus was upon the loss of income by the wage-earner. This was not an unexpected initiating cause since these families have so little margin on which to work that the loss of even one day of pay was a serious matter. Mr. Werner's explanation of what happens is enlightening in this connection:

*Just being sick shouldn't get a family into a mess. The doctors have got things down so perfect that most things can't kill you today. But, goddamit, being sick does get you into a mess just because the minute you lose a day you lose almost a fifth of your pay check for that week. Look at us: I've been down with a grippe-pneumonia for nine days and we're smack-bang in trouble. Why? Because the eighteen dollars I've been able to save in the last three months had to go to buy groceries and pay for the medicines the doc ordered. And the rent's due this week, too. Lucky my wife could get some work for the wealthy people over on Madison Avenue and save that money or we'd have to stall the landlord. And I'm lucky to have my job held for me, some fellows wouldn't even have that break. They say we ought to have insurance against this: sure we should, but where the hell's the money coming from to buy insurance? My family gets along all right—we don't have any mix-ups because I'm laid up—we take it in our stride, but Jesus, we certainly get balled up on eatin' and rentin' when that pay envelope stops!*

The holdover of trouble from illness of the wage-earner is illustrated by the Graves family situation:

*Look at us now. It's twelve—no, thirteen weeks since I was laid up with the "flu," and we're still trying to pay our way out of that trouble. I was laid up an even two weeks, and that meant a sixteen dollar doctor bill added on to the cost of living. It wiped out our thirty dollar savings and we've been eating light ever since, trying to get everything paid up. Why if I hadn't been "trusted" at the store up there on the corner, we'd had our choice: starving or goin' on the relief, and God knows, I wouldn't want to do that if it was the last thing to do.*

It is this holdover, with the necessity for operating at less than the usual minimum level of financial income that makes troubles in these families. With few exceptions all of these families tried to remain solvent—to be able to maintain as a reserve the little credit this subculture affords, only to be thrown seriously behind by even a few days of illness of the wage-earner.

(c) Resulting from poor management

The twelve troubles of a financial nature resulting from poor management fell into a common pattern. In all of these the problem was one of no member recognizing the lack of management, yet all being concerned with the financial problems which resulted. It is one thing to attempt to remain solvent, quite another to realize that the insolvency was caused by bad management on the part of the family.

In the Grosz family, where no one knew how to use money to the best advantage, trouble recurred at intervals, was always due to the same initiating cause, and always recurred again. The mother explained it in these words:

*It does seem that we can't keep from having spells of running behind. Albert's pay is always the same, but we do get behind.*

*Then we starve along and get caught up, but we do get behind
again, every time. I don't know why. We work together trying to
get caught up, and we work together to stay that way, but every
time we just can't manage, somehow.*

It seems paradoxical that bad management and a sense of responsibility go hand-in-hand in these three families. However, the demands of our money-centered culture are severe, the temptations to
spend money for things which attract the family are great, and inability to resist the latter in the face of the former results.

(d) Resulting from unemployment

In the one instance of unemployment as an initiating cause of
trouble, the pattern was little different from that shown above. The
significant fact here was that the Adrich family (*average*) was able
to face the trouble without being more seriously maladjusted. After
being unemployed for twelve weeks, during which time the family
lived off its savings (nearly two hundred dollars), and borrowed
from neighbors and friends, Mr. Adrich obtained another position
at a lower wage. After taking the new job, Mr. Adrich made the
following observation regarding his family's situation:

*Well, now, we had a pretty tough time, and more to come until
we get squared away again. But I tell you, the whole thing is outside our family—not inside: we don't always get along so well as
we might but we stuck together this time. I owe everybody and
his cousin except the devil, and we've been in plenty of a jamb,
but we'll make it out o.k.*

The significance of these troubles lies in the fact that debt was an
enemy common to the family as a whole, even in those families
which were *below-average*. None of these families were subject to
inter-personal problems as a result of the debt situations.

*Inter-Personal Problems*:

The fifteen initiating causes which resulted in seventy-three
troubles were, unlike those discussed above, all of a type affecting
the inter-personal relationships in the family. The ways in which
these set troubles in motion follow:

(a) Resulting from acute illness

Unlike the financial problems due to illness discussed above, the focus in these twenty-six troubles was on the structure of the family, not on its financial relation to the outside world.

There were three distinct sources of trouble in this group. In most of these situations, the illness was not that of the wage-earner but of the wife or other member, and one which required adjustments in the roles of the families. In the Guenther family, for example, the mother was ill with osteomyelitis and hospitalized for many weeks. The family income continued, and the cost of the hospitalization was born by the city, but the trouble for the family lay in managing the home while the mother was hospitalized. The father and twelve year-old daughter carried on the activities of the home, with some help from the neighbors. The problems resulting from the necessary temporary shift in roles was described by Mr. Guenther in the following words:

> We've really got trouble now, not money trouble, but real just the same. With Martha in the hospital, we're damned hard up to manage. I can't stay home from work, because we've got to have the money to live on, but I try to do what I can before I leave at seven in the morning, and what I can't do then just has to wait 'til I get back at night. Mary takes care of June 'til she has to go to school at eight-thirty, then one of the neighbors keeps June 'til Mary gets home at noon and feeds them what I've left in the morning. Then some neighbor keeps June 'til Mary gets home after school, and so we get on. The problem is kind of tough for all of us—I know June's unhappy being pushed around from neighbor to neighbor, and Mary's school work suffers, but we just have to put up with it 'til Mother's home again. This being sick can be pretty tough on a family! All this extra doesn't help my work, I can tell you that. But there's lot's worse off than us, so why kick. If only there was somebody you could get in at a time like this!

The serious disruption of family routine, whether the sick person was in the hospital or at home, presented the most serious troubles in this inter-personal group. It was this disruption which caused so many of these families to say "We can stand almost anything better than having somebody in the family sick." Illness in any home is disrupting—in the substandard home, the problem becomes even more acute.

Trouble also occurred where there was a culture pattern preventing adequate medical care. With the old-world culture pattern still dominant in many foreign-born parents (especially where the father was foreign-born), illness threw the family into trouble. The fear of doctors and hospitals was present in a number of families, and in four trouble situations, the father's attitude made illness more than an exigency. In the Eduardo family, when the daughter became ill with pneumonia, the father at first refused to allow her to be taken to the hospital. The son, sixteen years old, described the situation in these words:

*Agnes is sick and we all know she'd be better off in the hospital. We could pay for that, and everything'd be all right. But, Holy Mother, the old man won't let her go. He says they only kill people in hospitals, so we're trying to get along with her at home. If he wasn't such a stubborn old bastard we wouldn't have all of this trouble.*

Trouble resulted from illness, too, when it was related to a violation of the family's norms for itself—the gonorrheal infection of the son in the Czabot family is an example. The illness itself might well have been handled without its becoming a trouble had there not been the violation of the family's normative behavior.

(b) Resulting from chronic illness

Chronic illness, the initiating cause in five troubles, was even more important in its effect upon the family. It promised, in most cases, to be of long duration and with no hopeful prognosis, and in most cases it demanded the *permanent* readjustment of the family to the situation. For example, when the father in the Botaccio family became ill with diabetes and failed to respond to insulin therapy sufficiently to return to work, roles had to be relinquished and new ones assumed. The result was trouble—which involved every member of the family. Mrs. Botaccio's statement shows the confusion which such a situation brought into the family:

> Oh, we're so upset. Now that the Mister can't work no more (the clinic says he'll never be any better) we're all off the track. Joe [the 18 year-old son] has to go to work so we can live, and if he ever gets married, I don't know what we'll do. I guess Marie will have to leave school. Do you think Bloomingdale's will hire her at seventeen? Maybe we'll have to move to Cherry Street, it's cheaper there. This is so bad for us—why did we ever deserve such things? There isn't anything we can do, though, that I see—just go along and pray to the good Mother of Christ, Virgin Mary, to help us. Maybe she'll send us help.

Chronic illness, where it affected not the breadwinner but another member of the family, operated in much the same way except that it presented a different focus for the problem. In the former type, the problem was one of assumption of the breadwinner role; here the problem focused upon the assumption of other roles. In the Weingarten family, the father depicted his trouble in these words:

> The fix we're in is sure one hell of a fix. Heda can't ever really do anything again. The doctor says her heart is too bad—she has to stay in bed most of the time, and all that. That's really bad for us, because we have to work out some way to care for her and the three kids. I can't do it alone—we're here all alone and can't ask the neighbors to do anything. Two weeks ago life was going like glass; now we're certainly in a jamb. And nobody to turn to for help. Now I wish all our relations lived here.

(c) Resulting from mental illness

In one family an earlier trouble had resulted from a post-partum psychosis, with the mother hospitalized for eighteen months. The mother became pregnant again, accidentally, and an ill-advised staff psychiatrist in the hospital's out-patient department had assured the family that a second psychosis of the same type was probably inevitable.[6]

6. The writer has been assured by psychiatrists that this was very unlikely; in fact, no documentation of such a recurrence could be found in the literature.

(d) Resulting from alcoholism

One family, in which the father had been a steady drinker from adolescence, and who had systematically drunk up a fourth or more of his week's wages each Saturday night since his marriage, finally reached the trouble point when he began to drink so heavily that he would not appear at home for days, and the family was deprived of his income.

(e) Resulting from legitimate pregnancy

The wife's discovery of her pregnancy was the initiating cause of trouble in four families. All had a full complement of children (according to their plans) and two were families in which supposedly adequate contraceptive measures had been taken.[7] A secondary effect, in one of the families, was due to the violation of Catholic law regarding contraception—a violation which had been rationalized adequately until this "punishment of God" appeared, which in turn gave further emotional content to the situation since that statement by the father engendered further guilt feelings on the part of the mother.

(f) Resulting from illegitimate pregnancy

The family's discovery of the 16 year-old daughter's illegitimate pregnancy initiated trouble in the Grady family. While the negative social values in the situation were important, the focus of the trouble lay in the daughter's violation of the Church's teachings, and not in the problem of caring for the girl or her child. The father's successful effort to have the child aborted provided an additional focus of trouble within the same situation (which was not considered separately in Table VIII).

(g) Resulting from husband-wife conflict

Seven troubles, five of them in *below-average* and two in *average* families, were due to husband-wife conflicts. In these families frustrations were always present, and tensions rose and fell as the fortunes of the families varied. It was impossible to specify an exact condition in the environment or a specific occurrence in the family's

7. Both, incidentally, had depended upon nostrums purchased by advice of a druggist in the neighborhood.

life as initiating the trouble; the assignment of husband-wife conflict as *the* initiating cause was therefore arbitrary.

(h) Resulting from parent-child conflict

In the families where the organization was determined to be *average* or *below-average* and parent-child conflict had made necessary such an assignment, such conflicts initiated trouble.

In the Zarysk family the rebellion of the children against the demands of the parents was ordinarily not sufficient to cause trouble. When a special anniversary party was planned by the dancing club, however, and the father and mother insisted that the children attend, they rebelled openly, with a trouble resulting. The son's account of this situation follows:

> We've always went because we had to, even if we didn't want to. But this time I said No, we wouldn't go, that the settlement had a party we wanted to go to and Sara and I are old enough to do what we want to. So now we're in a hell of a mess. They won't speak to us unless they have to. They're both so mad at us we don't even get decent food to eat, just throwed at us. We sure got into trouble standing up for our own rights.

(i) Resulting from sexual incompatibility

Where there were conflicts in the family due to sexual incompatibility, trouble was initiated when the husband secured (or was believed to have secured) sexual satisfaction outside the marital union.

In the Barber family, the husband and wife were in a state of conflict due primarily to their sexual maladjustment. When Mr. Barber sought out a prostitute in the next block, which he admitted doing at intervals, trouble was initiated:

> When he goes to that bitch—I'd like to tear her eyes out—it just makes me see red. I know we can't get along that way—I just can't have him sleep with me. But I see red every time I know he goes to her, and then everything goes wrong here in the family. Even if he doesn't go to her as often as I think he does, it still upsets things when I think he's going there. If he stays out at night,

*I'm always sure that's where he is, and then I can't stand it—
things just bust up. We'd get along all right if it wasn't for that,
we get along between times, it's only when I get to knowing what
he does that way that we get in a jamb.*

(j) Resulting from death in the family

The nine deaths which occurred among these families in the two-
year period resulted in nine troubles. Only one of these initiated a
trouble which was inter-personal.[8]

In the Walther family, the death of the breadwinner placed the
responsibility for family support upon the eighteen year-old son, who
left school and took a shipping clerk's job in order to support his
mother and two sisters. Because of his new position in the family
as breadwinner, the son felt himself entitled to the headship of the
family, which the mother refused to accept. Their attitudes are
shown in the following quotations from the mother's and son's accounts of the situation.

> *Now that John is dead and Ernst is earning our living, he thinks
> he should be able to say what our family should do. He tries to
> make me let the girls do things their father never would let them
> do, and he's always telling me we have to live different and be
> different. I can't let him do this—just because he earns the money
> doesn't give him the right to be the boss. My husband was the
> boss—that's all right—but he's only my son. I can't keep us from
> having a fuss, I can't let him do the way he wants to with all of us.*

> *It's a hell of a note. Here I earn all of the money and support
> Mom and the girls and don't even keep out money from my pay
> for myself. And then when I try to have some say about how we
> live, Mom raises hell with me, treats me like a little boy. If I'm a
> man and taking care of my family, haven't I a right to say some-*

8. It is recognized that such a statement would not be acceptable to Eliot,
Becker, Waller, and others who have studied the psycho-social consequences
of death in the family, and to whom death is far more than an exigency. It
would be ridiculous to assume that in the eight families with trouble reported
as resulting from the death-debt sequence there had been no inter-personal disturbances. However, the focus of the present study was such that these emotional disturbances were considered to be among the exigencies of life that
affect all people and are excluded here for that reason.

*thing at least about how things go? Jeez, what's the use? I might*
*as well go away for all I have to say here.*

The result for this family was a trouble—a trouble which was resolved only through the continued pressure by the son and the two
daughters which overwhelmed the mother's striving to hold the
dominant position in the family.

(k) Resulting from the addition of a grandparent to family

In one family, when Mrs. Mark's mother was taken into the family because another family could no longer care for her, trouble was
initiated. The grandmother immediately began to "side" with her
daughter against the son-in-law in small matters which would have
been resolved under other circumstances, and trouble resulted.

(l) Resulting from indebtedness

Where the family became involved financially and the parents
were in conflict over the debt, a trouble was initiated. In three families, one *average* and two *below-average*, this situation presented
itself. The Bricker family's situation was typical:

Mr. Bricker could not resist a bargain, whether it be in razor
blades from a street vendor or in an over-stuffed chair which could
be had on a dollar-a-week plan from a cheap furniture store. The
home was full of odds-and-ends purchased by Mr. Bricker on such a
basis. As a result the family was indebted to everyone who had or
would give them credit. Mrs. Bricker's account of the inter-personal
relation which resulted is of value here:

> *Owing money doesn't bother Jim a bit, but I get so mixed up*
> *inside I can't stand it. I don't feel that I dare answer the door*
> *buzzer, because it'll be some collector with a court notice. Jim's*
> *been in court ever so often, but it doesn't bother him a bit. I get*
> *so I can't stand it and then I raise the devil around here. Then he*
> *straightens out a while, but we're always right back again. We'd*
> *be all right if it wasn't for that.*

(m) Resulting from conflict with neighbors

In one family conflict with the neighbors initiated a trouble on
the inter-personal level.

In the Corbin family, Mrs. Corbin was constantly quarreling with the neighbors on any excuse. Mr. Corbin did not share her animosity toward the neighbors and his attempts to keep Mrs. Corbin from disturbing the neighborhood invariably initiated a trouble within their own family.

*I'm getting so goddam tired of trying to be decent in this neighborhood. We had to move before because Berta raised hell with the neighbors all of the time, and I guess we'll have to move again. I don't mind that so much as what happens here anytime I try to straighten things out. Then she raises hell with me, and we don't get along worth anything for a while. Christ, sometimes it's awful around here.*

(n) Resulting from an educational problem

The need for the child to have more education was generally recognized in these families, despite the difficulties of providing such education. When the parents could not provide the financial support to allow the child to go on in school, a trouble was precipitated on an inter-personal level.

(o) Resulting from the international situation

With Mussolini in his prime in the early days of the study, and with many foreign-born Italians regarding him as "the saviour of Italy," trouble was twice precipitated in one family because the second generation was not in agreement with the father's feeling toward *Il Duce.* Mrs. Zucci's statement is self-explanatory:

*We are in such much a fix again. Nobody speaks to nobody. The kids, they laugh at Mussolini and fight my old man. He calls them sonsabitches and bastards. Holy Mother, they can't be in the house together. We don't even listen to the Italian music on the radio anymore. Papa shouts "Viva Mussolini," and then the kids they swear at him, and—oh, it's awful. If the Virgin Mother doesn't answer my prayers soon, somebody'll kill somebody else, sure. This happened before once, but the priest got them fixed up. Now it's worse than before.*

With these initiating causes and kinds of trouble, what steps did the families take to meet their troubles? To whom did they turn? The next chapter is devoted to a consideration of this topic, after which succeeding chapters will discuss the intra- and inter-family changes which result from trouble.

# CHAPTER FIVE

# The Solution of Troubles

*It ain't having jambs that's so bad. It's getting rid of the damn mix-ups you get into, and the not knowin' where to turn next, that gets you down.*

TROUBLES don't cast their shadows before them, in most instances. The research worker studying the life of the family or the social worker treating its problems may see premonitory symptoms of troubles in some instances, but for the most part, to the family at least, they drop like lightning from the sky. Caught in its own worries, bogged down by the exigencies of urban existence, and confused by the changing scene about it, the family knows only that yesterday it got along without too much difficulty and today it faces what appears to be a solid wall of trouble. What does the family do under such circumstances?

The ways in which these families solved or did not solve their one hundred and nine troubles may best be considered from two angles —in relation to institutional aids, and in terms of their own efforts, independent of help from organized sources.

### SOLVING PROBLEMS WITH INSTITUTIONAL AIDS

There are four general types of situations to be considered under this heading: (1) where no help was available from a social agency; (2) where help was available for a particular kind of trouble but the existence of such sources was unknown to the family; (3) where help was available and known to the family but rejected for one reason or another; and (4) where help was available and accepted.

Theoretically, at least, there were no situations which could be assigned the first of these. The social agencies of a city as well-organized as New York provided, apparently, for every possible contingency.[1] Readily accessible to the people of this block were social agencies meeting every need which urban man conceivably could have, regardless of race or creed.

It was impossible, of course, to determine whether or not any given trouble would have been solved by one or another agency; this could have been done only if the family's problem had been submitted to the agencies themselves. One can only judge by the statements of purpose of some of the leading agencies whether or not the family might have expected help, and whether or not social agencies are prepared to serve all families. The following statements of purpose are those of agencies active in the city area in which the study was made:

"The primary purpose . . . is service to individuals and families having problems which interfere with satisfactory and wholesome living. The service aims to help families overcome such obstacles to effective management of their own affairs as may be presented by financial strains, occupational handicaps, mental and physical illness, disturbed relationships." [2]

"To relieve at once acute distress and suffering: . . ." [3]

"By helping people in the early stages of their troubles, by sustaining them through periods of stress, by the provision of resources. . . ." [4]

From these generous statements of purpose it seems reasonable to assume that assistance was certainly available for such troubles as were experienced.

To determine whether or not families knew of agencies which might help in solving troubles, a check list was prepared containing

1. The Welfare Council listed in 1940 approximately 1000 agencies organized to meet the social welfare needs of the community. *The Directory of Social Agencies, New York,* 1940 (New York: Columbia University Press, 1940).

2. *Ibid.,* page 287.     3. *Ibid.,* page 286.     4. *Ibid.,* page 289.

the names of all agencies within a radius of one mile which offered service in the fields of health, family service, relief, day care of children, legal aid, loans, nursing services, and recreation. The families were asked, at the end of the study, to identify the agencies, to tell their approximate location, and to indicate whether or not they had ever had any contacts with them. The results of this survey are summarized in Table IX.

The widespread knowledge of the existence of health agencies, and the use of their services at least once by fifty-seven of the sixty-two families was not surprising, since illness presented problems which could not be solved without recourse to medical facilities. The five families which had not used any of the health facilities had all employed private physicians.

TABLE IX

*Number of Families Identifying and Contacting Specified Types of Social Agencies*

| Type of Service Rendered by Agencies | Number of Families | |
|---|---|---|
| | Identifying at least one agency | Having had contact with at least one |
| Health | 62 | 57 |
| Family Service | 27 | 5 |
| Relief | 57 | 19 |
| Day Care of Children | 3 | 1 |
| Legal Aid * | — | — |
| Loan agency (private) * | 1 | 1 |
| Nursing service | 43 | 12 |
| Recreation | 62 | 53 |

* Not within one mile radius.

Thirty-four of the fifty-seven families which had used the health agencies did not use them, however, *except in case of extreme need.* A summary of the opinions of these thirty-four families indicates that they considered medical clinics and hospitals impersonal, and rejected them on this basis:

*They don't really care about you there [in the out-patient clinics]. If you're something special the young docs can learn from, you're o.k. and get a break. If you're ordinary sick, they just push you through.*

*I saw the doctor eight times—he had to look at my card every time to call me by name. I didn't mean nothing to him. It was my liver he was interested in, not me.*

*Hurry, hurry, hurry—the nurse is always pushing you along, because there's somebody else behind you. You can't be last in line and if you are, then the doctor is in a hurry. The nurse acts like you are in the way.*

*What I don't like is the way they do it. Pay your money, do this, do that. It isn't like seeing a doctor, it's like being in a machine shop. You go in one end and click right along, only with a lot of waiting in between.*[5]

The widespread recognition of and use of recreational facilities (settlements, neighborhood houses, and the like) was also not surprising. Since their contacts with individuals ramify through all age groups, it was difficult for a family not to have known of and had some contact with one of these agencies. Also, the services rendered by these agencies were so varied and encompassed such numbers of people, both for regular and special events, that a family could hardly have lived in such total isolation as not to have known of at least one such agency.

The services offered informally by the personnel of these agencies were so varied *and so easily obtained* that families turned to them readily. The following, for example, were services given by members of one neighborhood house on one week-day: the loan of money for a "permanent" (to a girl about to graduate from high school), the use of the telephone, arranging a dental appointment, pulling a loose tooth for a seven year-old, translation of a letter from German into English and *vice versa*, settling an argument over health regulations, interpreting the draft regulations to the parents of a seventeen-year-old, helping a family to get an undertaker, lending a boy carfare

5. These statements are included to show something of the attitude of the patient toward the hospitals and clinics. It was reported to the writer that nearly half of the appointments made for or by people in this area with clinics and out-patient departments were broken without notice. The impersonal disinterest in the patient as an individual may well be a major cause of this absenteeism.

to and from a prospective part-time job, and so on. The workers in this agency were also called upon to listen to complaints, to settle quarrels, to share joys, and even to act as god-parents. The families which made use of the settlement facilities regarded the personnel not as professional workers but rather as fortunately-placed friends. The families which did not use these facilities were either closely joined in a family group, active in religious organizations to the exclusion of all others, or lacked understanding of what they might gain from such agencies.

The relief agency (the Department of Public Welfare of New York City) was well-known, fifty-seven of the families identifying it by name and locating the division office approximately. Nineteen families had, prior to the study, either received relief or had applied for it and been found ineligible. When the extent of relief in the depression years is taken into account, neither of these figures seems disproportionate.

The nursing services in the area were well-known, having been identified by forty-three families. This was to be expected, since the distinctive uniform of the Henry Street Visiting Nurses Association was seen daily on the block. Only twelve families had ever used this service—a smaller number than might be expected—but discussion with the families revealed that there was no objection to the service or its personnel. There was entire satisfaction on the part of those who had used the service—only inertia on the part of those who had not.

In the Botaccio family, where the work of a visiting nurse would not have prevented the trouble but would probably have eased it, the point of view is representative of this latter group:

> *I don't know why we didn't get her in [the Henry Street Nurse]. We get all mixed up, we don't think about her—she's a stranger, we don't have strangers in our house, and our house, it ain't too good, anyway. Besides, you hate to have to depend on somebody else.*

Here again the "you hate to have to depend upon somebody else" idea prevails, and the stigma attached to needing "help" prevents the use of what institutionalized aids the culture has already set up.

Facilities for day care of children were known to only three families, and had been used by only one in the past. Most of the families were surprised to learn of such facilities, which was due probably to their use as a resource for other social agencies.

Facilities for legal aid and for privately-run, non-profit lending agencies were least well-known. Not one family realized that it had recourse to civil law without paying for a lawyer. Only one family knew of the existence of the Hebrew Free Loan Association, and that family had twice borrowed money for emergency purposes. The Provident Loan Association was unknown to this group, probably because these families had little or no suitable collateral.

Agencies in the one remaining category, family services, were known to twenty-seven but used by only five families.[6] The statements of purpose given earlier are those of the family service agencies, and recognition of them by less than half the families, and use by only one-twelfth, brings sharply into focus certain questions regarding the relation of these agencies to the families in the study. Two primary questions are: why do more families not know of the existence of agencies intended for their use?, and, why do more families which do know of their existence not turn to them in time of trouble? Some information was gained from the twenty-two families knowing of but not using the services which helps to answer the second question.

A major reason in fourteen of the families was the rejection of such assistance as "charity." Material relief was objectionable to these families, although some of them had been forced to accept relief in depression days, and there was degradation in such acceptance. "Aren't we supposed to stand on our own two feet in America?" While the stigma appears to have lessened in time of depression, it returned with the official closing of that period. To these families there was no appreciable difference between the social worker giving a grocery order in 1936 and a social case worker giving

6. Nineteen of these twenty-seven families were Catholic and knew only of the Catholic agency.

case work service in 1942. It had been "charity" in the past; ergo, it was still "charity," and anyone who used the services of such an agency was "a charity case." [7]

The remaining eight families rejected the idea of assistance from a social agency on the ground that "social workers are Mr. Buttinskis," as Mr. Derber expressed it. As the family agencies have turned from relief-giving to the adjustment of human relations they have leaned heavily upon the findings of dynamic psychology, and have found it necessary to search for the causes of surface maladjustments in the inner recesses of the personality. This requires, legitimately, an investigation of the less-obvious relationships in the family, and it was this probing which created resentment of the social worker. Not, of course, that these families had been subjected to such probings, but rather that they feared such would be the case if they were to apply to an agency for assistance.[8] In all fairness it must be said that not one of these eight families could define its objections to the family agencies; all, however, were specific regarding their not allowing social workers to interfere with their personal lives.

A question asserts itself at this point: why, in a culture which demands so much and makes available so few institutional aids for family troubles, does this culture not provide a framework for these services which is acceptable to the families?

Little need be said of the families which sought and received assistance from social agencies. Having once met the eligibility requirements, and having accepted the methods of a social agency, the

7. This, of course, is far from the actual situation. With some exceptions, private family agencies have relinquished their relief-giving functions to public agencies (except as a temporary expedient where it is secondary to other problems), and the better private agencies have tended to concentrate their energies on family problems involving inter-personal relationships and on problems involving adjustment to the community.

8. Previously, two families in the block (neither in the study group) had experienced such investigations, both apparently at the hands of not-too-skilled workers, and their publicizing of the "snoopiness" of the agency had been effective in conditioning other families against the agency. The diffusion of such anti-agency attitudes, which is probably more prevalent than is generally realized, is worth some research itself since the meeting of families' needs is hampered thereby.

family was assured of help.[9] As will be discussed in the next chapter, the need appears to be not so much for services as for techniques in presenting the services and in bringing them to the people who need them.

### SOLVING PROBLEMS WITHOUT INSTITUTIONAL AIDS

While these families did not turn readily to family agencies, this does not mean that help and advice were not sought outside the family circle. To whom did they go for advice? In the one hundred and nine troubles observed, advice was sought from a number of informal sources.[10] Table X shows the sources from which such information was sought in fifty-seven of these troubles. In the other fifty-two, the family "muddled through" without seeking outside help.

TABLE X

*Number of Times Advice Was Sought from Specified Sources in Connection with Fifty-seven Specific Emergencies*

| Source of Information | Times Consulted † |
|---|---|
| Relatives | 36 |
| Druggist | 31 |
| Bartender | 29 |
| Priest * | 12 |
| Labor Leader | 6 |
| Political leader | 4 |
| Clergyman * | 4 |
| Policeman | 2 |
| Total | 124 |

* 38 families were active Catholics, 7 were Protestant church members, 11 were nominally Protestant, and 6 were unaffiliated.

† Advice was sought from more than one source in many instances.

It was not surprising that families turned to relatives more times than to any other individual source of aid, since they were in some measure familiar with the family's problems. The attitude which

9. These families' problems occurred prior to the study period, and the agency records were not made available to the writer. For this reason any discussion of the family problem and attitudes toward the agencies involved would be only one-sided.

10. As used here the word *advice* means the definite seeking out of an individual for help in determining a course of action; it does not mean the casual pouring out of one's troubles.

prevailed in the twenty-nine families which consulted relatives is shown in a statement by Mrs. Brees:

> *After all, what are relatives for? Blood is thicker than water. If you can't turn to your own blood, who live the same as you do, and know how hard it is to get along, who can you turn to? I know some people can't turn to their folks, but they ain't much folks in my opinion.*

There were exceptions, however, which are important. The Czabot family, faced with the violation of its norms, would not go near relatives, despite the fact that they could have been of real help. Where there were inter-personal problems initiating the trouble, as in the Rogers family, the relatives in the next block were avoided.

> *I know my uncle could help us straighten this out, but I certainly can't have him see this jamb we're in. You can't let your relatives know you've failed.*

The use of the neighborhood druggist as a source of advice for twenty-six families with thirty-one troubles was not unexpected. One has only to realize the aloneness of many of these families (despite the fact that they have friends and relatives) to understand their grasping at the nearest "authoritative" (but anonymous) source of information. To many of these families the druggist was an authority on countless small health matters—from belly-aches to corns—and his authoritative status carried over into non-medical matters. He was educated—his diploma and state license, prominently displayed, were evidence of this—and it was natural that to many he should be a guide and counsellor.[11] The families which asked his advice were distributed among all three types of adequacy; he was a source of information for most of the residents of this block. It happened that this particular druggist was an exceptionally high-type man, well-versed in human understanding, and with a

11. That the druggist is a source of information in matters of sickness has been shown before. For example, see Paul B. Gillen, *A Social Survey of Health and Illness in Urban Families* (New York: Cornell University Medical College, 1945).

sense of responsibility, and his advice—while not always good—was rarely harmful. The place he filled in the lives of some of these families is indicated in the following quotation:

> *We don't mind talking with Mr. ——. He never blabs what we say, and he's always ready to be your friend-in-need. Sometimes you don't know where to turn, you're so mixed up and nobody to get advice from, so you go talk to him and just telling him helps. It's just having somebody who seems to care that helps. I don't know why he listens—he doesn't make a lot of money out of my family, but he'll always listen. Sometimes he can tell you what you ought to do* [Gregory].

"Mac," the bartender in the corner tavern, was another important source of advice. Less learned than his neighbor, the druggist, he nevertheless was always ready with advice. Not always ethical advice—one could, if he knew the inquirer well, get advice on abortion techniques, on contraceptive measures, on inter-personal relations— he would even lend small amounts of money without interest if he knew the would-be borrower's credit was good—but again here was a friendly, personal source of information when confusion and sheer ignorance prevented one's knowing what to do or where to turn when in trouble.[12]

The priest was a source of advice in twelve and the minister in four troubles. With thirty-eight Catholic families experiencing sixty-seven troubles, and with the Confessional so important to the Catholic, this seems an untapped source of help. With eighteen Protestant families, and advice sought in only four troubles (two of these in one family) the clergy seems equally unimportant as a source of advice and help. The fact that the clergy, whether Catholic or Protestant, were in a measure removed from the vicissitudes of life affected their use as advisors in time of trouble.

12. Much could be said concerning the community organization of a culture in which only five families in a group of sixty-two turned to a social agency when in need of advice while thirty-one sought the help of the neighborhood druggist and twenty-nine that of the bartender in the corner tavern.

*What does he [the priest] know about jambs? He's fat and well-fed and hasn't got to face up to the kind of thing we do. As a religious man, sure, he's all right, and he's got his place. But it takes lots more than prayer and Hail Mary's in times like these. I can't go to him with my problems. He tells me to be patient and pray. I don't need that, I need to know what to do!*

*Our pastor is a good man, and he lives a good life, but I know he doesn't really know how I feel about not knowing what to do. If he really had to live the way we do, he'd understand better. But even in thin times he does pretty well. He doesn't know what life's problems are. How can he be a real help? Our pastor in Germany was one of us, he lived close to us in our village. Here he is away from us, and doesn't understand.*

Here again is the aloneness of living—even one's pastor, one's spiritual advisor, was aloof and not prepared to understand.

Half the troubles required money for their solution. The community provides only two opportunities for borrowing, other than from banks or loan companies: the Hebrew Free Loan Association and the Provident Loan Association.[13] Means of borrowing money were not unknown, despite the lack of agencies and ignorance of those which did exist. If only a small amount was needed, and there seemed certainty that the money could be repaid, it was often borrowed from relatives or friends, although the families reported that such sources of funds were no longer as plentiful as in pre-depression years. Where only a few dollars were needed, and the family had credit at the neighborhood stores, it was often possible to borrow from the storekeeper, have it "put on the bill," and pay an extra fifty cents for the privilege.[14]

13. The Hebrew Free Loan Association lends money without interest and without regard for race or creed to individuals who can show a reasonable expectation of repayment and who can provide two co-signers. The Provident Loan Association is an organization which lends money without usury on collateral such as silverware, cameras, etc.

14. This was understood by both parties to be illegal, but "you never look a gift horse in the mouth."

If one or more members of the family had steady jobs and the co-signers could be obtained, personal finance loans were obtained *at maximum rates.* The use of pawnshops and the "six-for-five" and "jewelry loan racket" have already been referred to.[15] Three families had been able to make loans on the cash value of small insurance policies to tide them over in time of trouble.

Despite the fact that money was important in half of these troubles, in that the problem might not have been precipitated or would have been eased had the families had more adequate resources, the real lack seems to have been in not "knowing how to deal with things as they come along."

What can be done? Is this one of the inevitable results of big-city life? Is it something the urban, industrial culture creates and which must be accepted along with depressions and the other uncertainties of our "American way of life"? What is the need in the future?

15. *Cf.* Ch. II.

CHAPTER SIX

# The Intra-Family Effects of Troubles

IT WAS mentioned in Chapter Three that there was no real balance of power in these families; that they were essentially patriarchal, that is, husband-dominant.[1] The grounds upon which this patriarchal pattern was accepted were of three kinds: *institutional*, with the traditional acceptance of the husband's authority; *personal*, with acceptance because of the wife's love for or psychological need of her husband; and *instrumental*, with acceptance because of economic need or coercion by husband.

In general, the *better-than-average* families had less dominance by the father, due primarily to the recognition of and mutual acceptance of roles. Where these families did have a strong patriarchal pattern, it was due to personal, and to some extent, institutional grounds. This was well-illustrated in the Czabot family, where the mother discussed the patriarchal pattern in these words:

*Of course father is head of our family. I loved him very much when we married, and so did he, and we haven't changed a bit in all these years. Why, it wouldn't be our family if we didn't look up to him and depend on him. He's father, and our love—the children's and mine—makes us want him to be the boss. There's*

1. This finding differs from those of certain other studies of low-income families. For example, Komarovsky found that among 59 low-income urban families in New Jersey, 14 were wife-dominant and 23 had no clear-cut dominance by either. Vera Komarovsky, *The Unemployed Man and His Family* (New York: The Dryden Press, 1940).

*something else, too; any good family looks to its father to be the head, that's the way families are set up.*

The *below-average* had a higher degree of dominance by the father, and it resulted primarily from instrumental grounds. The latter is illustrated best in the Carver family, where Mrs. Carver described her husband's dominance in these words:

> I guess my husband runs our family more than most men do theirs. To tell you the truth, I don't like it, and I don't like it for the kids. But what can I do? He earns all the money we have, and I don't have anybody else to turn to, so I have to do what he says. The kids don't like it, either, but when they try to do what they want to, he beats them if he doesn't like it. When they grow up, I'm afraid there's going to be trouble. I did, at first, try to have my say, but he just beat me down [figuratively] every time I said anything, and I just got discouraged. I hope most women don't have to live this way.

The reasons for the patriarchal patterns in the *average* families varied, but were, in twenty-nine of the thirty-four families, primarily personal with an institutional undercurrent. In the other five *average* families, the basic reason was institutional with a subsidiary personal basis.

The importance of this patriarchal family structure, with a high degree of dominance by the father, is of importance here. The far-reaching effects of a strong dominance pattern in the family are indicated by Horkheimer:

> Of all the social institutions which make the individual receptive to the influence of authority, the family must be recognized as the most important. In its circle the individual experiences the impact of social forces. Through it he gets his conceptions of their intellectual and moral content. The family largely determines the role these forces play in the formation of his spiritual life. Moreover, the patriarchal structure of the modern family serves by its very nature as an important preparation for the acceptance or authority in society. . . . To be sure, it does not represent any

final and independent force, but is a part of the evolutionary process. The social relations which the family helps to preserve and strengthen, themselves constantly reproduce it.[2]

There is further importance to this study in the fact that the most frequent changes in families in time of trouble occurred in this matter of dominance. In other words, the end result of trouble, so far as intra-family effects were concerned, seemed to lie most often *in the area of authority in the family*. Although not well-stated, the following analysis of the result of trouble by Mr. Kreuger is enlightening in this connection:

> *It doesn't really matter what happens in your family about the money you bring home—you always get along, maybe by getting relief. The real problem in any jamb, is what happens to your standing with your wife and kids. You can earn less money, and get along, except that your wife and kids think less of you and pay less attention to you when you do earn less money.*

### CHANGES IN DOMINANCE

It is helpful at this point to introduce a device for showing changes in the dominance pattern of these families. Using the biological symbols ♂ and ♀ to represent the sexes, and designating the father and mother with the letters (F) and (M), and the siblings as (1), (2) and so on, in the order of birth, the family is represented by a rectilinear figure with sides and shape governed by the memberships and relative dominance of each member.[3] This relative

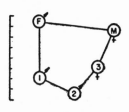

2. Max Horkheimer, *Studien über Autorität und Familie* (Paris: Felix Alean, 1936), p. 900. Quoted in Komarovsky, *idem*, pp. 3 f.

3. It must be understood that in every family each individual except one has *some* dominance, just as each member except one is subservient to one or more members. It is probably usual to think of *one* person as being *dominant*, but that is hardly realistic. True, not every member is involved in every sphere of family activity, but every member does have a place in the general picture of dominance in the family.

dominance of each member is indicated in relation to the positional scale at the left of the diagram. In the hypothetical family shown here, the father (F), mother (M), and siblings (1), (2), and (3), constitute the family. The father's position is dominant, the mother's position somewhat subservient to that of the father, next in line is the "baby" of the family (a girl), followed by the oldest son (1), and the second child, a son (2).

In this same family, if the mother occupied the dominant position

by virtue of her personality, by being the sole breadwinner, or for other reason, that fact would be indicated in diagram at left.

This device provides a means of showing graphically the dominance positions of the family at any time (in the present study prior to, during, and after trouble).[4]

Since troubles affect the dominance positions of various members of the family in different ways, each member of the family will be discussed separately.

### THE DOMINANCE OF THE FATHER

If, *in the opinion of the family,* the father failed to meet the demands of a trouble situation, a loss of dominance followed in every instance, regardless of the adequacy of the family. This is best illustrated in the Eduardo family, where the Italian-born father prevented the early hospitalization of the daughter, and in so doing, lost his dominance. The changes in dominance are shown in the following diagram:

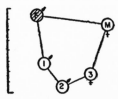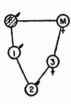

4. This same device might be used to show role devaluations in trouble. Since individuals have more than one role, and evaluations cannot be shown simultaneously for several roles without resorting to three dimensions, the device is confined here to dominance pattern changes.

The older son described this change in dominance in the following words:

> *The old man is always boss in our place. That's o.k., he's got a right to be the boss. But, Christ, he wasn't the boss after he belted that one around. When he raised hell and wouldn't let Agnes go to the hospital (and she sure was sick, too) everybody forgot he was the old man. None of us paid any attention to what he said. It was his own fault, he didn't need to be so goddam stubborn! Just because he's afraid of hospitals and what they do to you there. Yeah, he's boss again, but not the way he was before. If you didn't forget so easy, he'd never been boss again. If she'd a died, we'd have run him out of the house. Hell, he wasn't worth two cents in our family for a while.*

During the trouble period, the mother assumed the dominant position (headship) in this family, and this created additional confusion, since she was unaccustomed to such a responsibility. The oldest son (age 16) explained his own failure to assume the dominant position in the family in these words:

> *Well, I wasn't earning any money then, and besides, she's our mother, and we are used to doing what she tells us when the old man isn't around. You could take over when the old man flopped, but Mom didn't flop on this. It wasn't her fault Agnes didn't go to the hospital, so I couldn't take over from her.*

There was considerable evidence that the father in this family never quite regained his former level of dominance after this trouble. The daughter recovered, and less blame attached to the father's act than would have been the case had she died. This failure to prevent or to resolve the trouble was never completely overcome, at least in the following eighteen months of observation of the family. (This permanent loss of dominance is shown in the diagram, where the father's position has not quite its former distinct position.)

In other words, trouble apparently did cause permanent damage to the position of the father under such circumstances, with resulting damage to the family as a whole, since such a change meant that the stability of the family was shaken. The observation of Mrs. Derber on this point is of value:

> *It shakes your family when you know that the one strongest person of all—your husband—isn't able to handle the jambs you get into. You have to have somebody in the family to lean on, and when he fails you, if you think it's his fault, it busts something up.*

Also, where there were successive troubles, there was a cumulative effect. The Richmond family had a succession of troubles, all involving the husband's inability to keep out of debt, and Mrs. Richmond's observation is pertinent here:

> *Something happened, I don't know what, but every time you get in a jamb, when you get out you feel a little less sure about the person who caused it. Not that I don't love my husband, of course, but I begin to think maybe he's a little weak. Then next time I lose a little more of what I think of him, and so it goes again. When you think less of the person you think of as the corner [stone] of your family, it make the whole family unsteady, and you get a feeling, as a family, about things happening to you.*

It was this point which seemed the major (and tragic) effect of trouble in family life. With the family playing so great a part in the development of human personality, this effect of trouble in destroying the foundations upon which satisfactory interaction was based, *i.e.*, the security in each other, was of paramount importance to the individual members, whether they were directly affected by the trouble or not. A family is after all, love-in-action, which includes interest, respect, the chance for interaction, and so on, and this effect of trouble reduced measurably the chance for the working of all of them.

In some few instances, the dominance of the father was raised as a result of trouble.

In the Dickens family, where the husband's dominance over his wife was slight because of her aggressiveness (and in a measure because of his passivity), a serious trouble involving debt as a result of death was unexpectedly solved through the husband's efforts. As a result of his act, the wife suddenly found herself freed of worry over the situation, and his dominance was elevated markedly. His statement follows:

> *I never really knew until now what it means to be father in a family. Why, since my wife's attitude's changed, my kids are real different to me. The boy and I are real friends. Last week we went to the Bronx Zoo on Sunday, he and I, and we both felt good about it. It seems too bad we had to get into a jamb to have us feel like a family, doesn't it? I wish it could've happened five or six years ago—I'd of been a much better father to my kids, I know.*

The permanence of this elevation of dominance is indicated in the wife's statement *eleven* months later:

> *The Mister [she had always referred to him prior to the trouble as John, or more frequently as "he"] did something to all of us when he fixed that mess. He's never been the same since; it seems to me he's a bigger man. I don't know what to make of the change. Why, Jack and I think he's a much more important man than we did before. He's somebody to lean on* now!

"He's somebody to lean on *now!*" The strength and security for the family found in such a situation serves best to highlight the opposite effect, where trouble weakens and hamstrings the working of a satisfactory interaction which provides the *modus operandi* of adequate family life.

On the whole, however, in the one hundred and nine troubles experienced, the number of times the father's dominance was elevated was negligible. This was understandable, since the conditions in the culture were such as to inhibit rather than to assist in the solution of troubles.

Where there was no onus upon the father for the troubles, there were no changes observed in the dominance. Other effects of trouble upon the father's life in the family were observed, however, and are discussed below.

### THE DOMINANCE OF THE MOTHER

The shifts in the dominance of the mother were not comparable to those of the father. With some few exceptions, the mother was the pivotal person *around whom such changes occurred.* There were several reasons for this stability. First, the mother (unlike the father and the older children) tended to be less exposed to the vicissitudes of life. In the relatively sheltered position the mother occupied in these families (with their patriarchal pattern),[5] culture change, social conflict, and trouble affected the mother personally much less than other members of the family. As a result, her position was less affected than were those more directly exposed to the buffetings of trouble situations.

Second, the vulnerable position in these families was that of the individual who had to provide for the family and to make the major decisions, and whose dominance hinged, in some measure, on those two functions. The mother did not share this vulnerability and was therefore less subject to the impact of trouble.

That this was recognized, at least by some of the women, is indicated in this quotation from Mrs. Berger's discussion of her place in the family.

*It always seems to me so awful that the man has to take most of the rap when we get in a jamb. I'm here at home—the world goes by me. But he has to take everything right on his shoulders. It's unfair. I ought to share everything in times like these, but he's the one who is out in the world, and gets caught. He's the one the people call a failure if things go wrong.*

There appeared to be real value to the family in having the mother in this sheltered position, in that it provided the other members of the family with one person to whom they could turn for anchorage. Mr. Berger stated this fact in these words:

5. For an excellent statement of this position, see Howard Meredith's chapter on "The Character Implications of Marriage" in Moses Jung (ed.), *Modern Marriage*, (New York: Crofts and Company, 1940). Chapter XII.

*Mother [the wife] is really a god-send when we get into a jamb. She isn't out the way we are; the girl and I work and have to face the problem of trying to get along in our jobs and support the family and all. But Mother can stay at home and be sort of steady, and we can turn to her when things are pretty tough outside and know that she isn't so bothered by these things outside.*

### THE DOMINANCE OF THE CHILD

The children's roles in these families were subject to highly individualized definition, depending upon age, sex, sibling position, earning capacity, and so on. This individualization of roles, with accompanying variations in role evaluations, had an effect upon the child's place in the total pattern of dominance and made it difficult to place the child accurately in that pattern. For the same reasons, changes due to troubles were difficult to evaluate.

The small child was affected only indirectly by troubles. When dominance shifted, discipline often changed, and the smaller children were very often confused and bewildered by what went on about them in the course of trouble. One day father was *the* seat of authority, the one to whom to run when in doubt; the next day that seat of authority had shifted to another member of the family; later, father again seemed to have his old position back again. It was all confusing, but for the most part affected the child only indirectly.

In the case of the older children, more direct shifts were evidenced. In this series of families, it happened that the oldest male child was the one most affected by troubles; comparable circumstances might readily develop for older girls, except that in most of these families the girls were more protected than were the boys.

Where an act of the child initiated the trouble, a lowering of his position in the dominance pattern resulted. In the Czabot family, when the son became infected with gonorrhea, this was especially apparent. This youth had acquired a high position in the dominance pattern of his family, but when he became ill (both because his illness was due to a "dreadful disease" and because he had violated the norms of his family) his dominance position was depressed se-

verely, and at the close of the study had been only partially regained.
The diagram for this family follows:

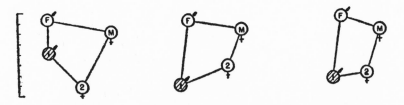

A compilation of his observations concerning his place in the
family follows:

> *My father and mother always treated me swell 'til this hap-*
> *pened. What hurts me is I didn't mean to do anything wrong, I*
> *got into a mess I couldn't seem to do anything about but go on*
> *with. So I got sick and then I had to tell my father. He was all right*
> *about it, took me to the doctor and helped me take care of myself,*
> *but he did change toward me. So did Mom when he told her. Sis*
> *has changed, too. She doesn't know what I did, or what happened*
> *to me, but she acts the way she does because Pop and Mom act*
> *cold to me. She knows there's something wrong. Pop and Mom*
> *sure changed, even if Pop did help me. I'm not really a part of our*
> *family now: I just seem to be an outsider. Something like the*
> *neighbor's boarder. He's in that family, but he isn't really part of*
> *it. Why, they don't even talk with me the way they used to. I*
> *don't feel as though I had any family now, just a place to stay and*
> *eat. . . .*
>
> *It's still pretty bad [six months later]. Oh, they talk with me,*
> *and we go places together now—we didn't for a while. But there's*
> *still a feeling that I don't belong. I try hard to be a part of the*
> *family, but they still hold back. They're fine—they really are, but*
> *there's something wrong. I just can't put my finger on it, but I*
> *know I lost something out of my life. I'd give most anything if I*
> *could do it over again and say "No" when I said "Yes" that*
> *time. . . .*

*I guess I'm back in the family, but I know it'll never be the same [fourteen months after the trouble].*

Corroboration of the boy's idea that the damage to his place in the family was permanent is found in a statement of the father one year after the trouble:

*Of course we've forgiven him, but after all, he broke his mother's heart and made us so ashamed of him, especially when the Krihak's found out about it, that somehow we can't get it out of our minds. I know he's all right again [physically], and learned his lesson—he'll never forget it, either—but that was our son who did it, and that's awfully hard to forget.*

That the reverse of this depression in dominance may occur was seen in several troubles involving older adolescents. Other things being equal, the older child knew more about the ways of the culture than did the parents. This was especially true in families where the parents were foreign-born.

In the Witlick family (both parents foreign-born), the eleven year-old daughter became ill with appendicitis, and as her condition became more serious, the father and mother passed from a state of confusion to one of panic. When the seventeen year-old son arrived home, he assumed control of the situation, called an ambulance, accompanied his sister to the hospital, and then cared for the parents until she was out of danger. From the hospital account, there is little question but that the girl would have died had he not acted promptly with decision. As a result of his action, his dominance position was greatly elevated, and, in the eleven months of observation of the family after this trouble, never returned to its previous lower level. The father made the following comment:

*We had never thought of John as growing up, we always treated him as a child 'til then. But suddenly, when Elsa and I couldn't do a thing, he was grown up—we had a man with us. Since then we are so proud of him—he's grown up! Why I took him to Bill's [a tavern], and bought him a drink and introduced him to the men there. He's a man now.*

### CHANGES IN VALENCE

The interest in changes of degree or of kind of valence in these families was relatively unproductive, primarily because exceptional degrees of such attachments were infrequent. In a few families, however, there was evidence of the development of special valences as a result of trouble.

Where the adolescent boy was instrumental in solving a trouble, a special attachment occurred between that individual and his father. This was not expected, since the solving of a trouble might well be a threat to the dominance of the father. The effect was exactly the opposite in the three families in which such a solution took place —instead of threatening the father, it brought about a heightened companionship and appreciation of the boy.[6]

### CHANGES IN ROLE EVALUATION

Role evaluation was defined in Chapter One as the "adequacy of the performance of the individual's rights and duties in his role as estimated by the other members of his family." In time of trouble, there appeared to be an inverse relation between responsibility for the action initiating the trouble and the evaluation of the individual's roles, but only where there was a real or implied responsibility for the initiating cause. The sharp division between troubles that are the *fault* of someone and those "that happen because we have to live the way we do" was again apparent in this connection. If an individual was responsible, in the opinion of the family at least, for the initiating cause of the trouble, he suffered a devaluation of his roles. *This devaluation was highly correlated, too, with changes in*

6. It seems likely that the sudden revelation of attained maturity (through providing the solution to a trouble) is akin to the planned-for initiation of boys into manhood in the simpler cultures. The wide diffusion of such ceremonies in primitive society suggests that when normal father-son relations obtain, it is "human" to welcome maturity rather than to resent it. There was considerable evidence that most of these fathers unconsciously welcomed their sons into manhood through the rite of buying them a drink or by some other public admission of their manhood. In the three families cited above, this rite was hastened as a result of the youth's part in solving a trouble.

dominance.[7] In the Eduardo family, for example, the depression in the father's dominance was directly accompanied by a role devaluation. In Mr. Eduardo's mind this was unjust:

> *I don't know how to make of it. I earn the same money I did before, I provide the goods for my family just the same, but they don't like it now the way they did. We're always poor, but they don't complain. Now, because they're mad with me about Agnes and the hospital, and don't pay no attention to what I say, now they don't like what I earn. I don't understand—I earn the same. But before, they're satisfied; now, they raise hell and tell me I'm a poor no-good-for-nothing. Now I catch hell both ways—no boss, no good for keeping the family.*

Mrs. Mergel illustrated this role devaluation accompanying changes in dominance in these words:

> *Maybe, it's too bad, I don't know, but when somebody in the family [talking of her husband] gets you in a jamb, you lose your faith in them a little and they don't seem as important in the family—but there's something else, too. What they did before [the quality of role performance] doesn't seem the same, even if it hasn't changed. I know we get disgusted with the things John does, if we're in a jamb, even if those things are just the same.*

The individual responsible for the initiating cause suffered twice, then, for his contribution to the family's insecurity; first in his loss of his place in the dominance pattern of his family, and again, in his loss of role evaluation. This was serious, in any family, since it affected the love-in-action which meant good family life; it was especially serious since it most often affected the key member of these patriarchal families, the father.

7. It is not always the case that role devaluations accompany changes in dominance. Dominance *may* be maintained (even though role devaluations occur) in cases where the dominance results from coercion or other means.

### CHANGES IN HOME ROUTINE

In time of trouble, in almost every instance, the home routine suffered. The clean, orderly home became a little less clean, less orderly—the never-too-clean home dirtier or more disordered. Troubles had, without question, a distracting and disorganizing influence. Mrs. Johnson, an exceptional housekeeper with great pride in her home and its condition, discussed it as follows:

> *I don't know why, but when we're upset or in a jamb, my house-keeping always is worse. It isn't just that I'm worried about what upsets us, but I'm worried about how it's going to hurt our family. I can't keep my mind on my regular work. Look at this place now. Why, I'm ashamed to have you see it. I don't see the dirt when we're in a jamb, that's all. And I know we let the children get away with things they couldn't do most of the time.* There are so many things happen to you when you get in a jamb.

It was in this realm of living that the young members of the family most often suffered. Without knowing what had happened or was happening to the family, they had to experience this disarrangement of living. The fourteen-year-old daughter in the Creighton family made the following observation regarding change in time of trouble:

> *Papa and Momma don't tell us when things are bad,* but I always know anyway. *Papa isn't himself, he doesn't help around the house, and Momma forgets a lot of things she usually does or makes me do. I can get out of practicing my music lesson, I can forget to dust my room, and when I can do that, I know something's wrong in our family.*

### CHANGES IN DISCIPLINE

Accompanying this relaxation in home routine was a frequent relaxation of discipline, as shown in the last previous quotation. The children, on the whole, "got away with more" when the parents were disturbed by troubles. During these events, some children went to movies which were ordinarily forbidden. In many families the hour for being in at night was less strictly enforced, or the choice of playmates was less strictly supervised. The preoccupation of the parents (and of the older children) with the trouble seemed to permeate all areas of living, with relaxed standards resulting.

The exception to this was found in those *below-average* homes where there was little supervision of the children. Here there was a heightened irritation, a tenseness that carried over into dealings with the children. In the Vlamen family, the thirteen-year-old boy made the following observation:

> *Jesus, do I catch it when anything's wrong around home. Holy Mother, I catch hell for anything. I can't even open my trap without getting my head taken off. When the old man and my mother are having some kind of mess, I sure stay the hell away. If I don't, I get you-know-what.*

### CHANGES IN SEX ACTIVITY

Two patterns of change in sex activity evidenced themselves in this group of families. Among those for whom the sex act had been a rich and satisfying emotional experience, the frequency of sex relations tended to be increased during trouble.

> *We seem to find help when we [have intercourse] while we are in a jamb. It makes you feel that your wife is sticking by you, and that you don't have to go it alone. I guess we had intercourse about every night when things were so bad. It was something to keep you through the day to know you had your wife to go to at night [Czabot].*

A single exception to this increased activity was found in the Riker family, where the wife made the following observation:

> *I always enjoyed that part of life very much, but since we've had this trouble, I can't seem to be roused the way I was before. As I've been disappointed (I know it's wicked for me to be, but I can't help it) in how John managed things, I've lost some of my urge. It's killed something in my spirit, I don't quite know what.*

Among the families for whom the sex act had always been more unemotional and perfunctory, there was a tendency to decrease the frequency during trouble.

*I don't know—when we have any trouble I don't bother the old lady. When you are in trouble, [sexual intercourse] just ain't worth the bother. She quit playing after we'd been married two years, and unless I ask her we just don't, and I don't think about asking her when I'm in a jamb.*

The wife's attitude in this latter group was well-stated in the words of Mrs. Wemer:

*I just don't seem to care about that anymore when we have trouble. It seems my mind is on other things and I can't accept it like I used to. So I say "No, please don't," when he asks me.*

There was, in all probability, considerable rationalization by this woman and by the others to whom the sex act (after the first few months of marriage, at least) was an unsatisfactory experience, either because of a fear of pregnancy or because of the unemotional quality of the relationship. The general impression gained was, however, that sex activity was diminished except where it was originally a rich, satisfying experience which gave special strength to the husband-wife relationship.

### THE TENURE OF TROUBLE

Directly related to the effect of trouble upon the family was the length of time that trouble continued. Table XI indicates the relation between the two.[8] It appears immediately that there is little relation between type of adjustment and tenure of trouble, since the

8. The tenure of the trouble was the length of time a family experienced other than its usual pattern of behavior. Several factors were considered in arriving at these figures: the length of time of temporary shifts in dominance or role evaluation, the period during which the usual family action patterns were disturbed, and so on. In some instances the appearance of a new trouble brought the first one to a close (for our purposes here). These figures cannot be regarded as definitive—they are introduced as indicators of the length of time a family remains upset as a result of trouble.

*better-than-average* families were upset for a longer period than were the *average* families. It should be remembered, however, that the troubles affecting the *better-than-average* families involved, in four instances, debt following death or illness, and in the Czabot family,

TABLE XI

*Tenure of Troubles, by Type of Adjustment*

| Number of Weeks | Total | Better-than-Average | Average | Below-Average |
|---|---|---|---|---|
| One or less | — | — | — | — |
| Two | 14 | — | 14 | — |
| Three | 9 | — | 9 | — |
| Four | 22 | 1 | 21 | — |
| Five | 9 | — | 7 | 2 |
| Six | 10 | 1 | 1 | 8 |
| Seven | 11 | 2 | 2 | 7 |
| Eight | 10 | — | 1 | 9 |
| More than eight | 24 | 1 | 7 | 16 |
| Totals | 109 | 5 | 62 | 42 |

personal problems resulting from the venereal infection of the son. All of these troubles were of such a nature that they required time in which to be resolved.

The difference between the *average* and the *below-average* families is striking. While more than two-thirds of the *average* families resolved their troubles within four weeks' time, none of the *below-average* were able to do so. More than one-third of the latter's troubles lasted more than eight weeks. This indicates that, for this small number of families at least, there was a definite inverse relation between the adequacy of organization and the length of time troubles affected the family. The importance of this will be seen in the next section.

THE PROFILE OF TROUBLE

Again it seems best to resort to a graphic device to indicate something of the structure of troubles. If the normal inter-action of the particular family being considered is represented by the dotted line *a–a'*, the point at which the initiating cause takes effect by *b*, the point to which the family inter-action drops in the depths of trouble by *c*, the point of recovery by *d* and the angle-of-recovery by *e*, a graphic description of the trouble may be had. It is obvious that a number of variations will be found: the decent from *b* to *c* may be less precipitous (if the "trouble" develops slowly; the recovery from *c* to *d* may be slow, making the angle of recovery *e* greater; the return to the original inter-action may not be to *a—a'*, if there is permanent damage from the trouble, but to a lower level. It may go,

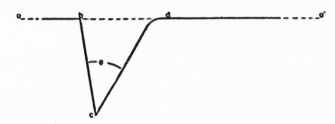

as in one family, to a level higher than *a–a'*, if the family is drawn into a tighter unity. There may, for one reason or another, never be an opportunity for the inter-action to return to the *a—a'* level, because of the impact of successive troubles.

There were approximately as many variations in the trouble profiles as there were families in the study, but they may be grouped in four general types, and will be discussed under these types.

The first profile is that for a family in which the inter-action returned approximately to its earlier level. In four of the five *better-than-average* families' troubles and in twenty-three of the *average*

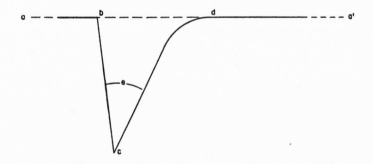

families' troubles, this profile (with minor variations) applies. The precipitousness and depth of the drop *b–c* and the angle-of-recovery *e* varied with the kind of trouble, the ability of the family to absorb shocks, and the speed with which it could dig itself out of the jamb.

For example, the Wilbur family had a very sudden depression of inter-action when they realized their financial problem; the reaction was severe because of the seriousness of the situation; the angle-of-recovery was very great because of the time and effort required to resolve the trouble. The family did, however, recover their original level of inter-action.

The Schumaker family, on the other hand, suffered a *gradual* depression of family inter-action as a result of the attenuating effect of illness in the family and recovered quickly when Mr. Schumaker's illness was unexpectedly cured and he was able to return to work with a resulting return to normal of the family's inter-action.

In general, these families can be characterized as having recovered to the pre-trouble level, but with variations due to the factors mentioned above.

The second profile is that for only one family in which the inter-action rose to a higher than pre-trouble level as a result of trouble.

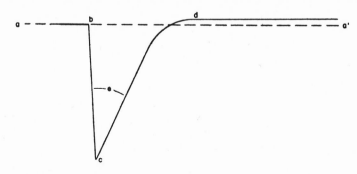

This was the Martin family (*average*) in which the inter-personal problem resulting from acute illness in the family brought, with its resolution, a better integration and more adequate facing-the-world-together relationship among its members. Mr. Martin's observation is of interest in this connection:

*It was the best thing that ever happened to us. Why, before the
sickness of the baby, we never were really together as a family.
Each of us sort of went his or her own way. We only thought of
each other as part of the family. But then when we had that jolt
and almost lost her, it did us a world of good. Why, now, we are
close together and couldn't think of each other except* as a family.

The fact that only one family benefited from its experience with
trouble is possibly a denial of that school of thought which regards
a family's troubles as something beneficial—as something that "tests
a family's mettle and welds it together." This may be the case in
middle or upper-class families; in this study it is certainly not demonstrated, nor does it seem likely that such is the case with most
low-income families. The constricting demands of the culture are
such as to nullify family inter-action rather than to develop
it.

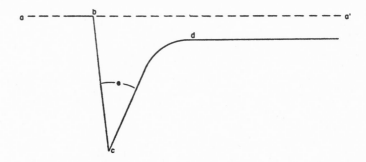

The third profile is that of a family in which the earlier inter-
action was not recovered fully as a result of trouble. One trouble in a
*better-than-average,* thirty-six in *average,* and twenty-four in *below-
average* families were included in this type. The post-trouble level
varied from family to family, and (in families with more than one
trouble) from trouble to trouble, depending upon the nature of the
initiating cause, but uniformly that level was below the pre-trouble
level. There was, for families of this type, lasting damage (at least
during the period of the study).

The fourth profile is that of twenty troubles in *average* families and six in *below-average* families. Here there was only incomplete recovery from one trouble before a second or even a third brought further erosion of the family's inter-action. In these families, it

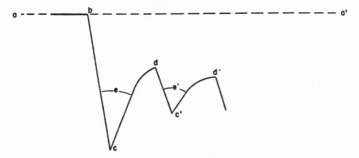

appeared that there was a successively-lessened ability to recover from the effects (shown in the greater angle of recovery *e′* than in *e*).

In summary, the results of trouble are as follows:

|  | Total | Better-than-Average | Average | Below-Average |
|---|---|---|---|---|
| First profile | 27 | 4 | 23 | — |
| Second profile | 1 | — | 1 | — |
| Third profile | 61 | 1 | 36 | 24 |
| Fourth profile | 20 | — | 2 | 18 |
|  | 109 | 5 | 62 | 42 |

From this it will be seen that one-fourth of the troubles occasioned no lasting change in inter-action, only one was beneficial to the family, and that three-fourths occasioned lasting damage to the inter-action of the family. The high frequency of the latter condition among the *below-average* families indicates the importance of adequate family organization if the family is to survive in the low-income environment.

It is in the latter two groups that the real tragedy of low-income urban life falls. Attempting to operate in a culture replete with handicaps and obstacles is a burdensome job for any family; when the lasting effects of troubles affording further handicaps, are super-imposed, it seems remarkable that these families survive without total disorganization.

# CHAPTER SEVEN

# The Inter-Family Effects of Trouble

W𝐇𝐀𝐓 happens to the family in its relation to the world outside the home when trouble occurs? Studies of unemployed families have shown that the family tends to withdraw from active contacts with the outside world.[1] Is the same true when the run-of-mine troubles in life occur, or is this withdrawal only a phenomenon accompanying depression?

For present purposes the informal friendships of the family must be considered separately from the more formal, organization memberships. These families had friends in varying numbers and with varying degrees of friendship.[2] The number of families considered as friends by these families is shown in Table XII.

For the most part these family friends lay outside the group being studied. They were distributed spatially throughout the city, but one hundred and seventy-one of the two hundred and sixteen families listed as friends lived within a radius of six city blocks. Despite the small number of families observed, there appears to be a real relationship between the degree of adequacy and the number of family friendships maintained. The average number of friendships per family is correlated with the type of adequacy, and the *better-than-*

1. Cf., for example, Paul F. Lazarfeld, *Die Arbeitslosen von Marienthal* (Leipzig: S. Herzel, 1933).
2. For the purposes of this study families were considered to be friends only if they maintained regular contacts, *i.e.*, visited in each other's homes or "did things together." The friendships of individuals within the family with other individuals outside were, for present purposes, excluded.

TABLE XII

Number of Family Friendships Maintained,
by Type of Adequacy

| | Total | Better-than-Average | Average | Below-Average |
|---|---|---|---|---|
| One | 7 | — | 3 | 4 |
| Two | 12 | 1 | 6 | 5 |
| Three | 17 | 1 | 14 | 2 |
| Four | 8 | 3 | 4 | 1 |
| Five | 5 | 3 | 1 | 1 |
| Six or more | 11 | 4 | 6 | 1 |
| Totals | 60 | 12 | 34 | 14 |
| Averages | 3.6 | 4.7 | 3.6 | 2.5 |

*average* and the *below-average* distributions virtually reverse each other. This suggests the fact, well-known to psychiatrists, that well-adjusted personalities make and maintain human relationships better than do less well-adjusted ones.

The organization memberships are shown in Table XIII. Here

TABLE XIII

Number of Formal Organization Affiliations of Adults,
by Type of Adequacy

| | Total | Better-than-Average | Average | Below-Average |
|---|---|---|---|---|
| Church | 32 | 4 | 26 | 2 |
| Social organization in church | 31 | 7 | 19 | 5 |
| School organization | 2 | 1 | 1 | — |
| Settlement club | 25 | 7 | 15 | 3 |
| Political club | 12 | 1 | 10 | 1 |
| Nationality club | 4 | 2 | 1 | 1 |
| Card club | 12 | — | 8 | 4 |
| Dance club | 3 | 1 | 2 | — |
| Sokol | 4 | 1 | 3 | — |
| Union | 21 | 6 | 11 | 4 |
| Fraternal order | 2 | 1 | 1 | — |
| Totals | 148 | 31 | 97 | 20 |
| Average | 2.47 | 2.58 | 2.88 | 1.43 |

again the correlation indicated in the earlier table is repeated, in that the *better-than-average* families had almost twice as many organization memberships as did the *below-average* families. (The greater average number of memberships [2.88] for *average* families is explained by the fact that a few families were very active in several organizations, thereby bringing up the average for the group.) Mrs. Hammer, for example, was a born "joiner," and had her family "joined to death," in her husband's words.

In the main, the friendships in the foreign-born families occurred among the members of the organizations to which the families belonged.[3] In the Berger family, for example, there were six friendships maintained; all of the six were members of the same Sokol and formed a small clique within that organization.[4] Mrs. Berger's explanation of the reason for forming friendships within a secondary group is interesting in this connection:

> *When you are young and first married you don't need friends so much. Then you begin to want them and of course it is natural to make them with the people who do the same things you do. We always went to the Sokol—our parents took us there—and it's easier to make your friends with people like yourselves. We do have some friends, not our best ones, who don't go to our Sokol, but we like to be with our own people. That doesn't mean that we don't visit our relatives, too; but they go to the Sokol, too, so we see them there. It's better if you get a little way from home when you get married, anyway.*

In two nationalities, however, consanguinity governed the friendship pattern of the families to a large degree. In general the Italian families, both foreign-born and native-born-of-foreign-born parents, made the greatest use of kinship in their friendships. The Ricci family's contacts were typical of this group and were described by the father in these words:

> *Our Sundays are our family days. Yes, we see our relatives other times, too, like on Saint's days, but Sundays we always go to my*

3. For a discussion of this distribution of friendship, which we have termed "the friendship pattern," see the writer's "A Study of the Use of the Friendship Pattern in Nutrition Education," in *The Problem of Changing Food Habits* (Washington: National Research Council, Vol. 108), pp. 74 ff.

4. A Sokol is a Czechoslovakian social organization, which emphasizes gymnastics and dancing, and which often is a drinking club as well.

*uncle's on Cherry St. It comes, I guess, from doing it in Calabria when I was a little boy. There, after Sunday dinner we always went to my grandfather's house. Here my uncle is the oldest and we just naturally go there. We talk, the kids play, we drink a little wine. It is the way we are brought up: to be a family. If you can't go, because you are sick or something, you feel something is wrong in your life until you can go again. It is the one way we can keep being Italian. We are American, yes, but it is good for us always to remember the good life of Calabria.*[5]

Where this type of friendship pattern operated, the number of social contacts with families not related to them was low. This had the effect of narrowing the social experience of the families, and confined their knowledge of social relationships to a very small area.

The Irish families followed the same general pattern except that their regular visits were most often to the homes of the maternal parents. The wife in the O'Brien family described their family contacts as follows:

*We always go to Mom's Thursdays nights. My two sisters bring our husbands and kids and visit. Mom always has tea and cake. It's then you tell the family you're preg—that you're going to have a baby, that Dan has got a raise, that the kid's tonsils have to come out. It's sort of like going to confession: you feel so good when you tell Mom and Pop everything. We go to Dan's family, too, only they live in Brooklyn now, and it's hard to get there. Gee, if you didn't have your family. . . . Well, it's nice to have friends, but they can't take the place of your own blood.*

The native-born families over-stepped nationality and organization boundaries more readily than did the foreign-born group. Also, the younger families were more likely to have residential propinquity as a basis of friendships, or their friendships were based upon

5. These foreign-born families, especially from the South and East of Europe, tended to idealize their European homes, probably because of nostalgia. The greater their disappointment in having been unable to achieve success and security in this country, the more idealistic seemed their regard for European family and village life.

chance acquaintance, *e.g.*, through continued attendance at a pre-natal or well-baby clinic. The Sylvester family illustrates the way in which such contacts were arrived at:

> *We didn't know people, we moved here from the Bronx to be nearer John's job. It's hard to get to know new people in a new place. We just lived alone and when baby was coming I went to the baby clinic. I went the same time every month and saw the same faces. After a while I talked with a girl my own age and found she lived across the street and that we were going to have our babies at the same time almost. So we'd meet after a while and talk. Nine months is a long time, you know. We walked home together and I asked her in and then she asked me over and by and by we were good friends. She came to see me when baby came and met John and when her boy came I went to see her and met her husband. We went to the well-baby clinic together afterward and that way learned to know Grace. Now we are the best of friends and the boys know each other and are good friends, too. They are the only friends John and I have.*[6]

Inter-family relationships were little affected by the activities of the children in these families. It was first believed that other or additional friendships might have resulted from the friendships formed by the children in school or at play, but this proved to be true in only one instance in one family. The establishment of and maintaining of the friendship pattern was a function of the adult members.

#### CHANGES IN RELATIONSHIPS DURING TROUBLE

The changes in these friendship patterns were directly related to *the adequacy of the family's organization and to the kind of trouble.* They could go on as before, they could retreat into a semi-seclusion and sever (for the time being) their social contacts, or they could increase their contacts to compensate for the trouble. Certain definite patterns of action were observed.

6. This account of how friendships are formed can be duplicated many times with only slight variations. It suggests that were such clinics not so formidable and thoroughly "professional" in most instances, they might render a genuine service in this respect.

The *below-average* families appeared, from the beginning, to suffer the least displacement of their inter-family contacts. While they had fewer of such contacts, those they did have were most often among families with similar characteristics.[7] There were, therefore, no sharp contrasts to make or suffer, and hence little reason to withdraw from social contacts because of trouble in the family.[8] In some of the *below-average* families there appeared to be a compensation for the impact of the trouble. The father in the Fratise family made the following statement regarding this stepped-up activity:

> *I think we do go out more—I know goddam well we do. You see, it's this way: what the hell, what have you got to lose? Everybody we know gets into trouble, you can't keep out of it, it's just human nature. Why, Christamighty, there ain't a family we know that don't get belted around plenty. So why should you stay home, just because something got mixed up? The old lady and I go more places when we're in a jamb than any other time. I ain't afraid to show myself to the world just 'cause I got a little trouble.*

Another function of this increased activity, at least for the few *below-average* families which were more sensitive than the Fratise family quoted above, was to provide them with diversion from the trouble. Mr. Corbin's statement shows this:

> *I think we go out together because we get away from our mix-ups that way. You get out, see your friends, play a little cards, maybe, and at least for the time you forget your situation. Not that it always works; you can't always forget a mix-up. It stays right with you even if you're playing cards. Why, last week we went to Burkes' to play hearts, thinking maybe we could forget*

7. From personal observation by the writer, and from descriptions of the friends and their activities, it can safely be said that *better-than-average* families consorted with families of their own level of organization, standards, and objectives, and that the *below-average* families consorted with families of similar characteristics.

8. It should be noted here that not many troubles remain secret from the neighbors. Tenement houses are notorious for their thin walls, which transmit sound (and seemingly, in some cases *ideas*) readily, and it is difficult to keep from having one's business known, or from knowing another's business.

*the mess we're in, but it kept staring me in the face all evening.
Hell, I lost twenty-seven cents—just because I couldn't keep my
mind on the game. Might as well have stayed at home.*

A second pattern of behavior exhibited itself, however, in these
*below-average* families in trouble. There was the chance that trouble
might be forgotten if it could be gotten away from:

> *I just had to get the hell away from home last night. I know
> we're all fouled up, and it's my fault; so I went down to Bill's place
> and had a few beers. At least you can leave your troubles behind
> you a little while, that way.*

The female counterpart of this "leaving your troubles at home" ex-
hibits itself in going out "for a good gossip." The wife of the man
quoted above (in the Mifflin family) characterized it in these words:

> *Yeah, the Mister goes down and has himself a few beers when
> he wants to forget some mess we're in. What do I do? Well, I go
> out to see some of my friends and pick all of the bones [gossip] in
> the neighborhood. There's nothing clears my head of a mess like
> hearin' all the dirt about somebody else!*

In sharp contrast to this brazen flaunting of trouble or attempting
to leave it behind to be forgotten temporarily is the behavior of the
four *better-than-average* families in which troubles were observed.
The effects of trouble were felt more keenly by these families, and
they had (in their own opinions) sharp comparisons to suffer. This
was true despite the fact that the troubles they suffered did not carry
connotations of personal blame or liability. As a result, they withdrew from most contacts with the outside world, and kept very much
to themselves. The thinking behind this withdrawal is illustrated
in these three quotations:

> *We wouldn't go out anywhere for anything! We're so ashamed
> of what has happened to us that we couldn't face anybody. Maybe
> they don't know about this trouble we're in, but it would always
> be between us and them as a wall.*

*We haven't been out anywhere since we got into this jamb. I think it's because we don't want to have to look at people who aren't in trouble.*

*You don't want the world to know you are in a jamb! So what do you do?—you stay at home and feel ashamed and do as good as you can. It might be better if you did go out, but Jesus, people always seem to know you're in trouble. You might as well carry a sign on your back!*

The feeling of having to be *ashamed* of trouble, whether caused by impersonal factors in the culture or by personal failure, is shown in all three of these quotations. It bears out the point made earlier that there is something shameful in our culture in having trouble, and that therefore it is something that must be kept hidden. At the very time the family needs help and the fostering of its social relations as a bulwark against the effects of trouble, the implication to the family is that it has "disgraced" itself and must hide away.

That such a reaction is not confined to the *better-than-average* families is shown in the experience of the *average* families. In the sixty-two troubles experienced by the twenty-eight families in this group, forty-nine occasioned some withdrawal from friends. Mr. Hammer's observation is pertinent here:

*It doesn't matter if your friends do know about your being in a jamb, and don't think it's your fault, and don't blame you—you still don't feel right. You still feel you've got to hide your head. Why, when the depression was on around here, I wish you'd a seen this neighborhood. People acted like their tails was between their legs! You'd think it was something they was to blame for! I get so sick of people being ashamed, just because they're in a jamb; and then I act the same way myself, and cuss myself afterward for doing the way I do.*

Mrs. Guenther saw the problem in these words:

*I wish we could feel that we can face our friends when we are in some kind of a mix-up. I really feel that's when we need friends,*

*but that's just when we can't go to them. Oh, of course I don't
mean when somebody dies. That's different. Everybody expects
you then. But when something's gone wrong in your family, you
just feel you have to sort of hide away 'til it wears off.*

The culture "expects you" to show concern when there is death in
the family, but the culture also imposes barriers when troubles other
than death (troubles which can be more significant for family relationships, more destructive of human values) affect the family. In
the experience of these families, at least, one hides away when one
needs help the most.

Nor did the withdrawal affect only the relations with other families. There was a marked correlation between withdrawal from
friends and withdrawal from organization activities. This occurred
especially in the families where the friendships with other families
were mainly within the organization limits. Mrs. Kreuger stated the
reason clearly:

> *Naturally we can't go to our club. Why, we'd see the people
> there we are friends with outside the block. No, we couldn't go
> there any more than we can go to see our friends or ask them to
> come here. We're just as shut off from our meetings as we are
> from our friends.*

In the Czabot family, when "the word got around" concerning
the boy's infection with gonorrhea, the family withdrew, even from
church participation. This retirement was explained by the father in
the following words:

> *Our church stands against this kind of thing, and we can't face
> our church people with this hanging over us. This is a Cross we
> have to carry by ourselves. We couldn't face the congregation,
> even if it is hard to stay away. We can give up the settlement meet-
> ings, that's not hard, but we can hardly bear to stay away from
> services.*[9]

9. It should be mentioned, in fairness to the church, that both the minister
and some of his lay workers tried to keep this family from staying away during
this trouble period.

Here again one glimpses the aloneness of poor people in trouble. Religion fills a real need, in part because it is religion, but also because it offers the thing cities (despite their welfare agencies) fail as yet adequately to provide: an understanding, steadying source to which one can go to unlock the desperate loneliness of being alone in trouble.

Two families, both *average*, set up compensating activities during the trouble period—both used the movies and other impersonal activities in order to forget their immediate problems. The Busche family went to the movies almost every night for two weeks during the period when they expected to lose their household furniture—in fact, borrowed the money to be able to go. Mr. Busche explained this paradoxical situation in these words:

> *Crazy, isn't it? We're about to be thrown out of our house and have our furniture taken away, and then we borrow money to go to the movies. We've got to do something to forget, though, and you can't do it sitting around home; you don't get any help from sitting and looking at each other. So you go to the movies, and for a little while at least you can be somebody else and think something else.*

It will be recalled from Table VII in Chapter Four that the *below-average* families had more troubles, and the discussion in Chapter Six indicated that these families suffered more lasting damage, on the whole, than did the *better-than-average* families. Here one faces a major indictment of unorganized big-city living: the poor and the unfortunate become progressively more socially lost as they encounter succeeding misfortunes. The fact that in this chapter the *below-average* families brazen through their difficulties or sit them out in taverns or in gossip sessions in no way alleviates the problem. An added indictment of our institutional system and our American middle-class ideology is found in the fact that in the *better-than-average* and *average* families there was no "facing down" troubles but rather a penalizing retreat in the face of the problem.

These findings pose the problem: what is the future need? Can the culture do anything about this destructive effect of trouble on the family?

# CHAPTER EIGHT

# The Future Need

Wʜɪʟᴇ this study has dealt with a specific, localized group, the question insistently recurs: are the human beings in trouble on the East Side of New York City fundamentally different from human beings in the Middletowns of America? Certain of the troubles are unique; others would have been softened had they occurred in the small town with its closer neighborhood ties. Still others, the illegitimate pregnancy with its abortion, or the gonorrheal infection of the adolescent, might have increased in intensity in a small-town setting. If, however, one views these troubles as types of human experience, as types of life's abrupt disconnections, they become (in the judgment of the writer) very commonly human. Therefore, the need to institutionalize aids to people in such common human experiences becomes not a New York City problem, but an American problem. It is also a problem confined not to "poor people" and to organized charity, but one which extends to the middle class and one which involves *our basic conceptions regarding the structuring of our institutions.*

A study like the present one challenges the American ideology and the rationale of our institutional system. It challenges—from the point of view of human needs, of democracy, and of social efficiency—the central assumption of individualism: that persons and families can and should be left to take care of themselves in an industrial and urban culture such as ours. Furthermore, it challenges the casualness of liberal capitalism about the social organization of a population, that is, the assumption that the integration of a population into a "society" can be left to chance, again on the assumption—now discredited but still employed—that "people know what is good for them"—that they know where they need social organization and can be counted upon to build it when needed. It challenges, too, the whole framework of assumptions on which organized social work is built: the assumption that the world is divided into two kinds of people, those who *can* and those who *cannot* care for themselves, and that minimum aids are needed only to shore up the latter.

From the writer's two-year participation in the lives of these families comes a consciousness of certain local needs, all of which operate within the framework of the preceding paragraphs, and none of which apply solely to the local community. Whether it is Bangor, Maine; Pasadena, California; or one of the many Middletowns in between, the basic needs remain the same. They may vary in degree, of course, but fundamentally they do not differ greatly.

The preceding chapters have indicated that the family with adequate organization either suffers less from trouble or recovers more quickly from that trouble. Conversely, the family with individualized and dispersed interests suffers more frequently, for longer periods of time, and with a greater degree of permanent damage. A first need, if the effect of trouble is to be minimized, is the re-construction of the family as a family. This is *not* to be construed as saying that it is up to the family. Quite the opposite! As our industrial culture has provided the elements leading to family disintegration, so must that culture now provide (through social organization) for the reconstitution of the family. If there are values inherent in family life (and the evidence is too well-established to need repetition here), and the culture neglects to preserve these values, we can only expect further family breakdown with increased social disorganization.

Such a re-construction is presumably to be undertaken by the agencies whose professed concern is with people's social needs, the social agencies concerned with education, recreation, and character building. But their present activities in this direction are only the proverbial "drop in the bucket." [1] Not only are they the "drop in the bucket," but they are also usually incidental to the major programs of the agencies. It is now a matter of focusing attention upon Johnny, with incidental attention to his family; it must become a focus upon the family with the attention to Johnny only a part of the attention to the family as a whole.

That this requires a re-thinking of social organization objectives is obvious; it is obvious, too, from the preceding chapters, that our complacent acceptance of the present institutional set-up must be overcome, at whatever cost, if the needed job is to be done.

The preceding chapters have shown, also, that *if* social agencies (in this case the family service agencies) are prepared to offer the inclusive services claimed in their statements of purpose, this fact must be made known. As the culture has grown, both in size and complexity, families know less instead of more of the help they may expect to receive with their troubles. A fundamental characteristic of the social work philosophy, of the whole institutional organization of social work, must be abandoned in this connection. In the words of a practicing social worker in this area, "We of course cannot go looking for people to serve. We can only wait until they bring their problems to us." One immediately asks why this need be true in a culture the characteristics of which so obviously place the individual and the family at a disadvantage.[2] Since it is still a "disgrace" to be helped in our culture (except in the minds of an enlightened few) it becomes ever more necessary that the institution of social work overcome or compensate for this handicap under which the family labors. Social work can do so only by re-interpreting its services to the community and by making the community aware of its services. The latter is the most urgent need, in the opin-

1. As one observes the programs of such agencies in this area, the few attempts at "family nights" and "family open houses" which *are* held seem pitiful efforts to meet the need. The obvious success of the few attempts made in this direction indicates the filling of a need recognized by the families themselves.

2. That social work is *beginning* to recognize this obvious fault is evidenced by the current discussions among certain of the professional leaders of the need for "case finding."

ion of the writer. The re-interpretation must be thought through by the members of the institution, which is time consuming and involved. Letting the community know of its services requires far less moving of heaven and earth, and is something within reach of the agencies, singly and collectively. The real ignorance on the part of families of the presence and functions of agencies has been shown earlier. Surely so small an effort at acquainting people with the availability of services as a local directory would not violate the established ethics of the institution of social work, yet even this is rarely done.[3] If the culture, on the one hand, offers new services to meet new needs, or strengthens existing services, it must at the same time accept the responsibility for utilizing every channel to acquaint the needy with a knowledge of where and how needs can best be met. Social work publicity seems geared to acquainting the potential giver with reasons for his giving, rather than the needy with a knowledge of what is available for their use.[4]

The fact that these families indicated a wide knowledge of and acceptance of settlements and similar agencies, as contrasted with a lack of knowledge of and use of case work agencies, is indicative of still another problem. The settlements, from our observation, tend to accept people *at their own level of need*, and to operate from that base in providing services. Such agencies admittedly do not provide case work services, except in a few instances, yet their acceptability to the people is such that the case work services might well be incorporated into their total function, at least in a modified form. In this connection, it is well to think of the changes in the emphasis of case work. As the family agency has changed from being a dispenser of

3. City-wide directories, designed for social agencies and selling at five dollars a copy, are available but are hardly the answer. Neighborhood directories, so far as we know, have not been published *for the people* of an area. (These people welcomed the idea of a small, simply, widely-distributed and community-focused directory with only one aim—that of telling people "Where Help Can Be Obtained." The use of such a source book might well be the subject of further study in this field.)

4. An example is the series of carefully prepared broadcasts currently used by community organizations in promoting an understanding of social work. Obviously beamed at the middle and upper classes, they fail to appeal to those most needing an understanding of social work services.

relief to an organization concerned primarily with the adjustment of the personal problems of its clients, organized case work has in some measure lost sight of the need for its services in giving what may be called "simple advice." [5] There are, at the present time, few such agencies to which families willingly turn for help on the more superficial levels of life.

This phase of the whole problem of institutional aids goes far beyond "poor people," settlements, and case work agencies. Trouble, as has been said before, is no respecter of class. The need for aids for the middle-class family's troubles is equally great. The problem here, of course, is that the present-day characterizations of family agencies —a holdover from the days of "charity"—operate to prevent their utilization by other than the "poor." There is some doubt that the family agencies of today can slough off the stigma of "charity" in the near future, which leaves the culture only the choice of establishing new institutional aids for the middle class, or of providing duplications of present services under different names.[6]

A further challenge to our culture lies in the head-in-the-sand attitude toward education for family life. We operate, apparently, on the theory that marriages are made in heaven—we unfortunately disregard the necessity for their operating on earth. As one analyzes the training for family life available to these families (and, in general, to all families), it becomes increasingly clear that with the exception of some factual information on sex given to a few of the youth, and some isolated, ill-planned and tedious lectures on sub-

5. Collectively, social agencies disagree with this statement. It can hardly be denied, however, that present-day social work in the family field stresses its contribution as one of adjusting "the unadjusted," and, in so doing, does not stress the "brief service" case. Even in these "brief service" cases one gains information only on a *quid pro quo* basis, *i.e.*, one must be made a *case* before the needed information is given. The contrast is sharply drawn when one observes the way in which families approach agencies such as settlements for general information upon which to base decisions regarding the less involved difficulties of living. Where settlements have introduced case work services, there is most often criticism from the casework agencies.

6. Some family agencies are attempting to meet this need, both through fee systems and through direct appeals to the middle class to use their services. This, however, like some other aims of the social agencies, is for the most part advanced in theory but retarded in practice.

jects such as "How to Prevent Bed Wetting," the culture does little in preparing individuals for carrying on in adequate fashion the most fundamental group in society.

There are, increasingly, high school courses in home economics and family living, but the fact is that such courses (while representing an enlarged conception of home economics) are nonetheless taught in departments of home economics and reflect their origin. Home and family education is far more than is involved in courses in consumer education, budgeting, and the like. Topics like the psychology of family life, and family-community relations, are found in a discouragingly small number of school curriculae. The expansion of home economics into an area to deal with home and family life is a step in the right direction, but it greatly needs to add to its present offerings if it is to be effective in helping the economically disadvantaged families of the future to adjust to modern urban society.

Adult education, which takes many forms and which need not take place within school walls, is no longer an opportunistic offering of bits of isolated knowledge. Its techniques have been so developed that it is able to bring to a given population adequately organized material in fields such as this.[7] The plethora of organizations in the American culture certainly furnish means of initial access to people in this respect.[8]

Adult education, sex education, and the training of youth for family living, however, meet only a part of this need for strengthening the family in relation to its troubles. Increasingly, as we have seen, older children play more mature parts in the lives of these families, and increasingly they have a part in the solution of troubles. While the social sciences have had an important place in the school curriculum in recent years, they have for the most part concerned

7. We have only to look at the adult education programs in rural areas to realize how effective the techniques can be in making a whole population cognizant of new motives and new philosophies of life. Admittedly the urban conditions render the problem more difficult, but the work of Peyser in Brooklyn and of Covella in Benjamin Franklin High School in Manhattan are evidences of real possibilities in this field.

8. *Cf.* the writer's "Food In The Lives Of Our Neighbors" (District Health Committee, Kips Bay–Yorkville Health District, N.Y., 1943).

themselves with the various levels of public activity, and have dis-
regarded for the most part the community functions which have to
do with the students' life in their own communities, and with their
own personal and family problems. Most of the adolescents in this
group of families had a fairly accurate knowledge of how the city,
state, and federal governments functioned as regards elections, taxa-
tion, and the like. None of them had any accurate knowledge of
how the community organizations for social welfare functioned, or
the kinds of services they offered, or of how the family might seek
help in handling troubles. Surely, in a culture which demands so
much and makes so little provision for meeting these demands, it is
the task of that culture through its schools to provide youth, as
youth and as the future adults in family life, with a knowledge of
the important tools for better day-by-day living.

These needs are not impossible of fulfillment. They require no
new agencies. They do require, however, a new attitude on the part
of our institutionalized aids for family living. The onus is too easily
put upon the family—"We can't *make* people come to us for help"
—and the realization of the responsibility of the culture, through
the institutions it has set up, is lacking. The problem is not one of
setting up institutions and waiting for people to come to them when
in trouble; it is, rather, the problem of recognizing that in our involved, opportunistic culture we are faced with the real problem of
recognizing troubles as concomitants of that culture, and then of
proceeding on the basis that our institutionalized services must real-
istically approach those troubles in ways that can be acceptable to
members of that culture.

# APPENDIX

# Interviewing in This Study

IT HAS been a source of satisfaction to those concerned with this study that so high a percentage of families approached agreed to participate. The granting of repeated interviews by sixty-two out of a total of eighty-one families approached seems exceptional for such unprepared-for interviews.[1] This high rate is especially satisfactory in view of the highly personal nature of the present inquiry.

The literature on interviewing stresses the importance of certain qualifications on the part of the interviewer. For example, Professor Burgess indicates his belief in the following as essential:

> The primary requisite of the seeker after personal documents is a sense for the dramatic in all human life, a sympathy broad enough to encompass the manifold diverse manifestations of human nature, even those that are commonly regarded as shocking or even outrageous. My own experience as well as observation of the success and failure of students seems to show that the inhibitions to personal revelations are not generally so much in the

1. In the course of several years' work on this area—on this study, on studies for the Kips Bay–Yorkville District Health Committee, for the National Research Council's Committee on Food Habits, and for the Department of Public Health and Preventive Medicine in Cornell University's College of Medicine— the writer has approached without pre-arrangement more than 2000 families. In this total number the rate of acceptance varied with the subject matter and with different approaches but averaged not more than 55 acceptances per 100 approaches, as contrasted with a rate of about 76 per 100 approaches in the present study.

subject as in the attitude of the inquirer. Both this dramatic sense and this sympathetic attitude indispensable for success in securing personal documents naturally develop under favorable conditions but are also susceptible to special training for research work.[2]

His first requisite is of importance to this study, and one which must be challenged. The "sense for the dramatic" *has no place in studies like the present one*—it is this attention to the "colorful" which makes one suspicious of studies such as this. It is *not* the "dramatic" the research worker needs to focus upon, but the *humanly significant*. The latter may be the slow attrition of the feeling-tone between husband and wife, the subtle changing of role evaluations—nothing dramatic at all, but rather "life trickling away into the sands."

The "sympathy broad enough to encompass the manifold diverse manifestations of human nature" is quite a different matter. To this we not only cannot object, but must also stress its importance. The research worker who approaches a problem such as the present one can do so only if he exercises this sympathy to its utmost. But more must be done than exhibiting sympathy if research of this kind is to be carried out successfully. There must be an identification with the family which goes beyond any "sympathy." This, to the writer, is more important here than is any other single qualification of the interviewer.

We have already discussed in Chapter One the way in which this identification was obtained, and have indicated its importance to the family. In retrospect it seems that the ability to conduct repeated interviews on the level demanded by this study depended in large measure upon this *quid pro quo* identification with the participants.

There are, however, additional factors which appear to have been equally important to its success. The first of these is the peculiar focus of the study. The fact that anyone in a non-authoritative position was interested in one of the major concerns of the family—its

2. E. W. Burgess, "Statistics and Case Studies as Methods of Sociological Research," *Sociology and Social Research*, 12:118.

troubles—was enough to engage the interest of most of the individuals approached. Professional workers are of course interested in the troubles of this group, but it is an authoritative interest in the sense that people understand trouble to be the job of the social worker, and a job to be disposed of as quickly as possible. The contrast provided by an individual who had no authority and who readily admitted that it was really none of his business (except that he too had troubles and was interested in what people are to do about them) overcame much of the reluctance which ordinarily deters those interviewed.

Here, too, was the hunger of people to talk and the presence of someone *who was willing to listen.*[3] While conversations were guided, time was never allowed to seem important. So far as the family knew, the interviewer had unlimited time to devote to any one visit.[4] This leisurely participation in the family's discussions provided an opportunity for *katharsis* such as few individuals in these families had ever known. Such a technique made it possible, first, for the individual to talk out the locked-upness most humans experience, and to explore unconsciously the deep, anxious pockets of concern which low-income life engenders. The importance of this exploration cannot be overestimated as it applies to this study. The basic data from which the preceding findings were derived involve these underlying frustrations and these deep-seated concerns, and could hardly have been discerned had this technique not been adopted.

Also, the matter of being "a person with an opinion worth listening to" was obviously important. The low-income urban environment offers few chances for the individual to have recognition or

3. *Cf.* the experience of the Lynds in their first *Middletown* study where people said repeatedly that "they were hungry for a chance to talk and were so glad the interviewer had come" (from a personal communication).

4. The time spent on individual interviews ranged from a half hour to as much as three hours. Contrast this with the visits of the social investigator with a large case load and little time, who had constantly to interrupt with questions in order to cover her subject. One father characterized such visits in an earlier period of home relief as follows: "Damn it all, I never had a chance to *tell* her anything. She was always asking questions."

new experience, and small opportunities such as interviews bulk large in life as a result. By means of this listening technique the individuals felt themselves to be important enough to have their opinions sought, a unique experience in itself.[5]

The respondents also found emotional release through these interview processes; moods were very often given form and positive significance through the discussions, especially through those not bearing directly upon trouble situations. Here, in the person of the interviewer, was a new individual almost within the family circle; here were new horizons of thought, new sharings of the familiar scene.[6]

Since the original interpretation of the study to the families included the idea of using any findings for bettering the patterns of social service, their troubles might actually be of help to others in the future. This certainly was another unique idea to these families.[7]

A further factor in a study of this nature lies in the participant-observer nature of the technique. While it was hardly comparable to the anthropologist's living in a strange culture, it definitely had none of the get-in-get-the-information-get-out technique of the public opinion poll. The fact that the research worker came to know the families intimately and shared many personal and social experiences with them made the study a very genuine adventure in human relationships.[8]

5. One of the fathers said: "You feel great, don't you, when you can tell somebody something instead of always being told. That's the trouble with this world—you're always being told."

6. One evidence of this being "almost within the family circle" was in the more general problems families were apt to discuss with the interviewer. Quite apart from the study were many discussions which involved such questions as "Do you think Johnnie should go through high school? Is it worth our trying to do it?," "Do you think we ought to let Mary go out with the boys at eighteen?," and so on.

This bundling up of problems and dumping them into the "friend's" lap is a further evidence of the desire to break down the aloneness of life.

7. Cf. the experience of interviewer in the Komarovsky study, *op. cit.*, pp. 6–7.

8. In the course of the study at least one meal was eaten in the homes of more than twenty of the families; one wedding and many social events in the

It seems likely, too, that the sex of the interviewer had something to do with the adequacy of the technique. Male family heads are apt to resent it if family members other than themselves divulge information about family situations, at least until good rapport has been established. This rapport was apparently easier for a man to obtain than would have been the case with a woman research worker.[9] In the case of the women members of the family, most of whom are accustomed to men in the confidant relationship (the doctor, the priest, the minister), the same seemed to be true. The fact that most social workers (the only other people who enter the family for interviews) are women also probably operated to advantage here— no similarity of sex identified this as "social work."

Still another reason for success may lie in the fact that families of this class level have less "face" to lose than would middle-class families, and can possibly afford to be more frank under these circumstances.

The above discussion highlights one possible contribution to the body of information on interviewing techniques in that it stresses the need for highly personal relationships between the interviewer and the respondents in research studies of this nature. This point is neglected or treated only inferentially in the literature. If there is to be understanding of role devaluations, of changes in dominance, it can be secured only by interview contacts which have this highly personal quality.

The writer is conscious of the bias against the research worker's having other than a cool, impersonal relation to his respondents, and recognizes the dangers that are inherent in the more personal approach.[10] Every effort was made to guard against distortions aris-

---

neighborhood were attended, all upon direct invitation of one or another family. The climax of this participation was the invitation to attend a *paesano* celebration (a society of families from one village in Italy) which was usually not open to outsiders.

9. Much of the best interviewing of the fathers was done over a glass of beer in one or another tavern near the block.

10. While his criticisms are directed specifically against the life history, Read Bain's discussion of "The Validity of Life Histories and Diaries," in *The Journal of Educational Research*, 3:156–161, can be considered as representative of the criticisms directed against the intuitive procedures employed here.

ing from this approach. (It should be noted that repeated interviews, carried on over a long period of time, allow constant checking and rechecking against the intrusion of bias.)

If the interview is to yield anything beyond the most superficial observation, it cannot be carried on with the persons immersed in an icy apartness. Once having yielded this point, interviewing becomes a matter of candor with one's self and one's data. The demand for scientific objectivity in social science is responsible for this icy apartness, and makes such an approach *less* objective rather than more so because it leaves out of account the fact that human beings have emotions, and that emotions are in many situations a part of the data. To use techniques that detract from the possibility of getting this type of data is to detract from the hoped-for objectivity.

(One entirely personal observation may be permitted regarding a difficulty encountered in a study such as this. The research worker entering upon this study was forced, by the nature of the study, to deal objectively with a highly subjective subject matter. One of the real personal problems encountered was having to refrain from inciting the family to positive action in meeting a trouble. In almost every instance, help could have been made available to the family in solving its particular trouble, or at least in alleviating it. The frustrations resulting from being unable to help the family, because of the demands of the research situation, were great. Of such things are psychosomatic disturbances made.)